INAUTHENTIC
ARCHAEOLOGIES

INAUTHENTIC ARCHAEOLOGIES

Public Uses and Abuses of the Past

Troy Lovata

Left Coast
Press Inc.

Walnut Creek, California

LEFT COAST PRESS, INC.
1630 North Main Street, #400
Left Coast Walnut Creek, CA 94596
Press Inc. http://www.LCoastPress.com

ISBN-13: 978-1-59874-010-3 hardcover
ISBN-10: 1-59874-010-5 hardcover
ISBN-13: 978-1-59874-011-0 paperback
ISBN-10: 1-59874-011-3 paperback

Library of Congress Cataloging-in-Publication Data

Lovata, Troy, 1972-
        Inauthentic archaeologies : public uses and abuses of the past /
Troy Lovata.
            p. cm.
Includes bibliographical references and index.
        ISBN-13: 978-1-59874-010-3 (hardcover : alk. paper)
        ISBN-10: 1-59874-010-5 (hardcover : alk. paper)
        ISBN-13: 978-1-59874-011-0 (pbk. : alk. paper)
        ISBN-10: 1-59874-011-3 (pbk. : alk. paper)
1. Archaeology—Moral and ethical aspects.
2. Archaeology—Social aspects.
3. Authenticity (Philosophy)
4. Forgery.
5. Pseudoscience.
6. Archaeology—Philosophy. I. Title.
        CC175.L688 2007
        930.1—dc22

2006026627

Printed in the United States of America

∞™ The paper used in this publication meets the minimum requirements of American National Standard for Information Sciences—Permanence of Paper for Printed Library Materials, ANSI/NISO Z39.48–1992.

07 08 09 10 11   5 4 3 2 1

CONTENTS

Acknowledgments

Writing projects often seem, to both the author and the reader, to be solitary undertakings. Yet this book owes much to the many family, friends, and colleagues who made it possible. Specific thanks go to Elizabeth Bruinsma for her ideas about Stonehenge II; Todd Lovata for his invaluable editorial comments and assistance in mapping and measuring sites; Cornelius Holtorf for presenting me with examples of his work; historian and ranger Joseph Weixelman for sharing his doctoral research on the mystery of the Anasazi; Yorke Rowan for outlining his study of the Holy Land Experience and producing, along with Uzi Baram, the especially useful book *Marketing Heritage: Archaeology and the Consumption of the Past*; Trent de Boer, Jannie Loubser, Mitch Allen, and Eric Shanower—who all participated in the Comic Book and Cartoon Archaeology symposium at the Society of American Archaeology meeting in the spring of 2005 and offered invaluable insight into how people view the past; Charles T. Keally for providing information on the Japanese Paleolithic frauds; and my wife Diane for her input and unwavering support of my research.

CHAPTER 1
STUDYING INAUTHENTIC ARCHAEOLOGIES

Inauthentic archaeologies are indeed archaeology. Perfunctory dismissal of them as *only* pseudoscientific beliefs and forged artifacts is a failure to recognize their social roles. The inauthentic can still be meaningful to people engaging with the past. Yet authentic artifacts and sites are different from archaeological fakes, frauds, replicas, and re-creations. The differences vary because not all inauthentic archaeologies are the same. Inauthentic archaeology, like authentic archaeology, is context dependent. Study of inauthentic archaeologies helps us understand how archaeology operates and how the discipline affects people.

A First-Hand Introduction to Inauthentic Archaeology

The archaeological record is not confined to only a few special places in the world. Yet we need to know what we're looking at, and what we should be looking for, to see the variety of archaeology all around us. First-hand experience can be a key to this process. First-hand experiences with the archaeological record are often the most meaningful interactions that either professional archaeologists or the general public can have with the past. They can produce an epiphany or "ah-ha" moment that brings the past into perspective.

In the summer of 1996, I took a job as a crew member on an archaeological survey of a massive reservoir that bridges the American state of Texas and the Mexican state of Tamaulipas. The region was in the midst of a severe, multi-year drought, so the water level of Falcon Reservoir had dropped tens of meters for the first time in fifty years. Archaeologists had previously studied the area when this section of the Rio Grande was first dammed in the middle of the last century. Now receding water provided an opportunity to reexamine sites, gauge how sites had been impacted, and see what new archaeology had been uncovered after decades submerged.

Our crew spent the days systematically walking the newly exposed shoreline and marking the location of any artifacts we saw. This stretch of the border is sparsely settled today, yet we encountered a large number and a wide range of artifacts in our survey. It was not out of the ordinary to find a thousand-year-old Native American dart point the same day that I saw shards of glass bottles left by Mexican American ranchers only a hundred years ago. These individual finds would later be used to define entire sites. The federal law that initiated our survey stated that these sites must be at least fifty years old to be deemed significant—that is, significant enough to qualify for nomination to the National Register of Historic Places. Archaeologists uncover interesting artifacts and sites all the time that are less than fifty years old. But I was doing a government job that had very specific guidelines about what we recorded and what we ignored.

The vegetation around Falcon Reservoir had come back quickly after decades of being submerged. During my surveys, I walked across grassy pastures with only the husks of dead trees to remind me that quite recently I would have had to swim the same path. One morning, I reached the end of one such field and, under the shade of a fast-growing salt bush, I happened on a small pile of sharp stones. They were grey colored and fine grained and experience had taught me that they were a chert from central Texas. They weren't a tool themselves, but I saw that they could be pieced together. The flakes matched each other and had obviously come off the larger chunks. This was the debris left over from making a single stone tool. I congratulated myself for having found not just a set of artifacts, but a real archaeological rarity—a discrete site that encompassed a single instance of human behavior.

However, my enthusiasm had already started to wane by the time the rest of the crew arrived to admire the find. The artifacts clearly weren't half-buried. Instead, even the smallest flakes sat on the surface. Most sat atop the vegetation. This pile seemed just a little too tidy to be prehistoric. The crew spotted dusty footprints around the artifacts and noticed tire tracks nearby. Border smugglers, ranchers, recreational fisherman, and hunters frequented this area and had created a jumble of impromptu dirt roads across the newly dry lake bed. We also saw that the site lay on a low, but nonetheless scenic, prominence with a good view of the water. I noticed that I had taken advantage of the shade when I sat down to inspect the stones. And we all thought back to the local sportsmen, many of whom collected arrowheads. We thought about the large number of collectors who had become avid amateur archaeologists and tried their hand at flint knapping. Flint knapping is a popular pastime in Texas—there are clubs, organized competitions, and frequent demonstrations of how people had once made stone tools. Amateurs valued the high quality and easily attainable cherts from central Texas.

The entire crew agreed that I had found an interesting site but that it was of modern making and perhaps even less than a year old. It was certainly a fine example of the skill involved in working stone and it clearly showed us how to interpret the remains of lithic manufacturing. But it wasn't what we were looking for. It wasn't nearly old enough for our employer's fifty-year cut off. So we decided against marking the site. As we walked away, I thought about how the rains would eventually return to this section of the border. Then, in a year or two, the water level of the reservoir would rise again. I thought about how further down the line, perhaps in only fifty years, another once-in-a-century drought might pass this way again. I doubted this particular site would stay just intact enough for another archaeologist to next time find what they were looking for.

Judgments about Authenticity

Authenticity and its opposite, inauthenticity, are concepts that encompass a range of states. Both concepts are judgments based on the contexts in which things are experienced, considered, and presented. They encompass terms that range from real, genuine, accurate, valid, and verified to forged, faked, inaccurate, re-created, and replicated. These concepts are of use because they let us describe and demarcate the archaeological record. They are also valuable—perhaps more valuable—because they let us understand how archaeology operates. Judgments of authenticity and inauthenticity necessitate a contemplation of context that reveals the choices archaeologists and the wider public make and the reasons behind those choices. Understanding context is valuable because, as historian of archaeology Bruce Trigger (1989:380) has noted, the influence of society on the discipline "appears to remain one of archaeology's permanent features."

The use of authenticity to describe and define the archaeological record is similar to what art historians term *nominal* authenticity (Dutton 2003). This is the process of identifying and naming things. Nominal authenticity answers questions of classification and physical integrity. For instance, an art historian might determine—that is, authenticate—that an unsigned work of art was, in fact, created by the artist to which it is popularly credited. Archaeologists don't generally credit something to a particular person. Rather, they most often make judgments of nominal authenticity about specific attributes of artifacts, site morphology, or how material culture might relate to groups of people. For example, an archaeologist might use radiocarbon tests to attribute a firm date to burned fibers from a prehistoric burial. Another archaeologist might compare the decoration on a fragment of pottery to a reference collection or guide book and then deem it the product of a specific cultural group. Finally, still another archaeologist might examine a bone under a microscope and determine that a set of interesting scratches weren't made by people at all, but instead were the teeth marks of a scavenging porcupine.

Asking and Answering Meaningful Questions

Nominal authenticity obviously has a key role in archaeology. I made two such judgments—concerning age and cultural affiliation—when, first, I deemed the lithic manufacturing site at Falcon Reservoir to be product of human activity and, second, when I decided against officially recording it. My judgments allowed the crew to complete our survey and finish the job that we had been hired to do according the conditions laid out in federal law. There would have been a problem if we were unable to estimate the age or cultural affiliation of the objects we encountered. Without these kind of judgments, we would be endlessly walking—or, perhaps, swimming—the border today. But archaeologists should be aware of the limitations of simply naming or describing things. The act of labeling is dependent on our ability to discern the context in which things are deemed authentic or inauthentic.

Archaeologist Ian Hodder (2003) notes that students of archaeology must learn to identify artifacts to excavate correctly as well as make valid interpretations about what we find. For instance, there are serious problems if an archaeologist can't differentiate between the dirt surrounding the artifacts and mud bricks that are themselves artifacts. There are even more serious problems if an archaeologist is unable to place our work within a wider perspective. Hodder (2003:59) goes on to explain that if archaeologists, "do not look beyond the individual context or unit they are excavating, they will not be able to deal with interpretative issues that involve other contexts and other sets of data." Archaeologists must understand how the artifacts we uncover relate to entire sites, how such sites relate to other sites, and how all this material culture relates to actual people. Isolated facts and trivia about the past are not enough to constitute a discipline. Connections need to be made between contexts and facts because they operate in tandem. Philosopher Peter Kosso (2001:72), in his studies of the ways in which we come to know archaeology, explains that, "the necessity for negotiation between the content of a knowledge claim and its larger context, and the benefit of reciprocity between background knowledge and evidence, are key features in knowledge of both the facts and the values of the past."

It is more meaningful to understand why the laws that guided my survey of Falcon Reservoir had a fifty-year cut off than it is to simply determine whether something meets that minimum. What is implied by this standard? Are things that last at least this long significant because they've stood the test of time? Is a half-century enough time to step back from what past generations thought was important so contemporary archaeologists can more easily determine what's *not* worth saving? Or is a fifty-year deadline just an arbitrary, nicely round number that made its way into law and has little to do with the process of understanding the past? These are all questions about the contexts in which archaeology operates. Attempting to answer questions like these is a useful exercise for archaeologists in training. But they are also relevant for practicing archaeologists because the context of the discipline is not set at a single point and static thereafter. Archaeologists aren't just technicians who merely record data. Finds must be understood and interpreted in relation to past, current, and future contexts. Methodologies change because ways of understanding change.

Regulations Protecting Archaeology

Many different municipal, state, and federal laws protect the archaeological record in the United States. One key piece of legislation is the National Historic Preservation Act of 1966. It authorizes the secretary of the interior to keep a list, called the National Register of Historic Places, of districts, sites, buildings, structures, and objects significant in American history, architecture, archeology, engineering, and culture. Archaeological surveys are often conducted when federal property is affected by—or when federal money is used for—disruptive activities like construction. The archaeologists directing these surveys need some way to sort through the material culture they encounter. Archaeology sites are usually considered significant enough for further study, or even outright preservation, when they are eligible for inclusion on the National Register. The regulations that guide the National Register, known as at 36CRF60, specify that most archaeology needs to be at least fifty years old to be included. Understanding this regulation helps explain the contexts of, and reasons for, federal archaeological preservation. The relevant section of regulation reads as follows:

Sec. 60.4 Criteria for evaluation.

The criteria applied to evaluate properties (other than areas of the National Park System and National Historic Landmarks) for the National Register are listed below. These criteria are worded in a manner to provide for a wide diversity of resources. The following criteria shall be used in evaluating properties for nomination to the National Register, by NPS in reviewing nominations, and for evaluating National Register eligibility of properties. Guidance in applying the criteria is further discussed in the "How To" publications, Standards & Guidelines sheets and Keeper's opinions of the National Register. Such materials are available upon request. National Register criteria for evaluation. The quality of significance in American history, architecture, archeology, engineering, and culture is present in districts, sites, buildings, structures, and objects that possess integrity of location, design, setting, materials, workmanship, feeling, and association and

(a) that are associated with events that have made a significant contribution to the broad patterns of our history; or

(b) that are associated with the lives of persons significant in our past; or

(c) that embody the distinctive characteristics of a type, period, or method of construction, or that represent the work of a master, or that possess high artistic values, or that represent a significant and distinguishable entity whose components may lack individual distinction; or

(d) that have yielded, or may be likely to yield, information important in prehistory or history.

Criteria considerations.

Ordinarily cemeteries, birthplaces, or graves of historical figures, properties owned by religious institutions or used for religious purposes, structures that have been moved from their original locations, reconstructed historic buildings, properties primarily commemorative in nature, and properties that have achieved significance within the past 50 years shall not be considered eligible for the National Register. However, such properties will qualify if they are integral parts of districts that do meet the criteria of if they fall within the following categories:

(a) A religious property deriving primary significance from architectural or artistic distinction or historical importance; or

(b) A building or structure removed from its original location but which is significant primarily for architectural value, or which is the surviving structure most importantly associated with a historic person or event; or

(c) A birthplace or grave of a historical figure of outstanding importance if there is no appropriate site or building directly associated with his productive life.

(d) A cemetery which derives its primary significance from graves of persons of transcendent importance, from age, from distinctive design features, or from association with historic events; or

(e) A reconstructed building when accurately executed in a suitable environment and presented in a dignified manner as part of a restoration master plan, and when no other building or structure with the same association has survived; or

(f) A property primarily commemorative in intent if design, age, tradition, or symbolic value has invested it with its own exceptional significance; or

(g) A property achieving significance within the past 50 years if it is of exceptional importance. This exception is described further in NPS "How To" 2, entitled "How to Evaluate and Nominate Potential National Register Properties That Have Achieved Significance Within the Last 50 Years," which is available from the National Register of Historic Places Division, National Park Service, United States Department of the Interior, Washington, D.C. 20240.

Context Dependency

Most discussions of authenticity, in art as well as other fields like archaeology, directly or indirectly refer to the ideas of early twentieth-century-philosopher Walter Benjamin and his influential essay, "The Work of Art in the Age of Mechanical Reproduction" (1969). Benjamin postulated a hard line separating original works of art and their replicas. He argued that original works of art have an aura that mechanical reproductions lack. That aura is supposedly an inherent condition, endowed in original production, that permits an object to be deemed authentic. Benjamin made a significant point in highlighting not just the role of the artist in crafting a piece, but the role of the audience in viewing and consuming it. To him, aura was something felt by audiences in specific ways in specific circumstances. This is important because it means that modern-day people who interact with ancient material cultural have a role in those object's existence. Modern-day people are an audience to ancient artifacts. We can interpret artifacts and make meaningful statements about them, even though we didn't create or originally use them.

Scholars in a number of fields—including art, folklore, sociology, anthropology, and archaeology—have used, refined, and refuted various parts of Walter Benjamin's view of authenticity in the nearly seventy years since it was put forth. Some, like influential philosophers Umberto Eco (1986) and Jean Baudrillard (1994) continue to draw clear distinctions between the ways in which originals and reproductions affect people. Their visits to wax museums, American historical reproductions, and museum displays of Egyptian mummies led them to believe that replicas are degradations of the original. These scholars find simulated and replicated exhibitions without contextual reference and lacking nuance in the ways that Benjamin viewed reproduced art lacking aura. But other scholars disagree about how reproductions function and whether they do, in fact, lack reference.

Archaeologist Cornelius Holtorf (2005a) has persuasively argued that ideas of aura and authenticity are more context dependent in archaeology than Benjamin claimed for art. In fact, the aura of an artifact is not merely set during its production. The aura changes where and when it is observed. People are explicitly taught in educational settings—and implicitly taught through a succession of other experiences—to revere particular objects. They are revered for what they represent, for their age, for who crafted them, for what they are made of, for how they are made, and for who found them. For example, archaeologists negotiate authenticity and bestow aura when we discuss how an excavation was conducted. Professional methods and standards of archaeology must be met for artifacts and sites to avoid the taint of inauthenticity and instead be granted the aura of authenticity. The peer-review process and the open and frank presentation of one's work are two methods that most archaeologists depend on to advance our understanding of the past. We should also recognize that standards and professionalism change over time and in different places. For instance, Bruce Trigger's (1989:379) sweeping historical survey of the discipline of archaeology reveals that interpretations of archaeological evidence—which include the standards of what constitutes acceptable and quality practices—are often subtly influenced by social and personal preconceptions.

Contrary to Walter Benjamin's view, people's judgments of authenticity are context dependent to such a degree that people can find aura even in reproductions of artifacts. Cornelius Holtorf (2005a) provides several examples of museum-goers who don't realize they are seeing replicas or copies and nonetheless still experience the kind of aura of generated by original artifacts. These visitors implicitly trust the learned museum curators and archaeologists to present the originals, and their perceptions about authenticity followed accordingly. Aura in such cases is dependent on the context of the display: formal museum settings and curation labels signal that importance.

However, visitors aren't simply fooled by context. It's wrong to think that public audiences must be hoodwinked into experiencing fakes as real. The mere idea of an original can be just as valid as a physical example. Archaeologist William Lipe (2002) has observed that the tourists he brings to archaeology sites still have meaningful experiences when they know that they're looking at reproductions or reconstructions. Tourists expect them to be credible representations because they accept that archaeologists are skilled enough to correctly interpret finds and fill in the missing pieces of the past. Moreover, because objects are clearly labeled as reproductions—and, therefore, it is clear that no one is trying to fool anyone else—tourists have even more reason to trust and accept honest presentations. Visitors can have a transcendent experience with a reproduced past if they believe in the past being presented. It's not that visitors are unimpressed with original artifacts, it's that they're savvy enough to know that inauthentic objects can convey authentic ideas.

The Value of Studying Inauthentic Things

Archaeology students spend a tremendous amount of time learning to establish authenticity in order to work with the archaeological record in the field, laboratory and library. Acquiring an understanding of inauthentic objects extends an archaeologists' ability to work with the archaeological record into the public sphere: conference rooms, classrooms, the media, museum displays, and around the dinner table with family and friends. Because inauthenticity itself is a variable function of the context in which it is recognized, studies of inauthenticity are examinations of the environments in which the past is constructed and interpreted. A multiplicity of contexts demands a corresponding wide range of abilities. Archaeologists learn a jargon-filled patois to talk with each other. But archaeologists must also develop the skills needed to ask pertinent questions about broad, fundamental topics. We need to be able communicate with others and not just ourselves. Archaeologists like Trent de Boer (2004) have discovered that even discussing archaeology with dear and open-minded listeners—such one's own family or friends—requires context-specific skills and strategies.

Archaeology students first associate the inauthentic with hoaxes, forgeries, and faulty scientific claims. Academic discussions and public debates of archaeological authenticity are often framed as science versus pseudoscience. The debate surrounding the authenticity of the Kensington Runestone is one well-chronicled example (Cole et al. 1990; Michlovic 1990, 1991—the runestone itself is discussed in more detail in Chapter 3 of this book). Other examples are the work of archaeologists such as Stephen Williams (1991) and Kenneth Feder (2002), who have made meaningful contributions by writing explicitly about archaeology hoaxes and debunking pseudoscientific beliefs. Their books are popular with both academic and public audiences, and they take readers down interesting paths. It is enlightening to consider why someone might falsify artifacts or why people hold beliefs contrary to scientific evidence. It is enlightening to be shown logical inconsistencies and learn that gaps in people's knowledge affect their beliefs. But outright frauds and erroneous scientific theory are only two specific kinds of inauthentic archaeologies. Not all inauthentic archaeologies are the same, so their nuances are worth examining in detail.

Many archaeologists and archaeology textbooks have argued that the only way to react to inauthentic archaeologies is to prove

The Tübingen-Weilhelm Menhir and the Vasa Warship

Archaeologist Cornelius Holtorf (2005a) has observed two interesting examples—a menhir in Germany and a warship in Sweden—of people having meaningful experiences with, and finding aura in, the less-than-original artifacts that they encounter in museums.

Menhirs are tall and long stones that prehistoric peoples sat upright to mark the landscape. Construction in the late 1980s in Tübingen-Weilhelm, Germany, uncovered a massive menhir. Archaeologists moved this enormous rock to the State Museum of Württemburg in Stuttgart and, a few years later, erected a replica in place of the original. Weilhelm's locals know the stone left outdoors in their village isn't original, but few realize that the menhir put on display in Stuttgart is a replica as well. In fact, the original menhir was too heavy to be stored anywhere in the museum except the basement. So a second reproduction was created for the museum's visitors. Neither replacement menhir is marked as a replica. But, whereas people can and do knock on the replica in Weilhelm and feel that it's hollow, museum-goers customarily refrain from touching the displays and subsequently knowing the truth about that re-creation.

Sweden's Vasa Museum houses the Vasa, an immense warship that sank shortly after being launched from Stockholm in A.D. 1628. After the Vasa was raised from the ocean in 1961, archaeologists discovered that the ship's timbers had decomposed so far that each part wood contained eight parts water. An especially laborious preservation process—which took nearly twenty years—replaced the water with polyethylenglycol (PEG). Today the ship on display is mostly PEG and some of the associated artifacts are almost entirely made of this modern material. The display still has a powerful presence because the PEG successfully evokes the shape of the past. In contrast to the Tübingen-Weilhelm menhir, the Vasa's curators clearly explain the preservation and replacement process to museum-goers. Nonetheless, the museum remains an extremely popular attraction—it's the most visited museum in Scandinavia—and people feel a distinct aura when viewing the ship even though they know it's not entirely original.

them wrong and spread a contrary or corrective message (numerous examples of this process are listed in Holtorf 2005b and discussed in Michlovic 1990). Many archaeologists seem to have taken to exposing wrongs as something of a crusade in which all nonprofessionals, nonstandard practices, and nonscientific views of the past are targets. However, even archaeologists like Alice Kehoe—who is an ardent defender of science-based archaeology against pseudoscience—has noted that lumping different inauthentic archaeologies together is problematic for scholars. For example, she has observed that an inauthentic archaeology used to promote tourism and another based on discrediting the scientific establishment are founded and sustained in very different manners (see Cole et al. 1990:393). Subsequently, any archaeologist who studies or responds to them must analyze or react to each in their own way.

Of course, not all views of the past are equal, and it is completely acceptable to refute claims for which you have evidence to the contrary. But single-minded refutation, or even dismissal, is a blunt instrument for interacting with the nuanced relationships that people have with the past. Cornelius Holtorf (2005b:549) explains that:

> Different visions and experiences of the present constitute a range of contexts in which the past and its remains are given meaning. It is hardly appropriate to complain that people who are not professional archaeologists themselves may hold badly informed views of professional archaeology and have aspirations to interpret the past in other terms than those (most) professional archaeologists prefer. Instead these views and aspirations are significant in themselves: as different manifestations of a widespread fascination with both the past and archaeology.

To summarize Holtorf: students of archaeology should appreciate inauthentic things for what they *are* rather than what they *aren't*. Archaeologists who refute dubious accounts of the past are better served by understanding the contexts that shaped those accounts, instead of simply finding fault. They should ask questions about why people maintain the inauthentic or what people take from obviously inauthentic things that they can't get from authentic archaeologies. The best counter against something you disagree with is to create your own, more persuasive account in turn. But, of course, you must build from a solid foundation of what you know about the past as well as about the construction of archaeology itself. Holtorf (2005b:548) claims that when we find fault with stories of the past, rather than lodging critiques, "the only true remedy for professional archaeologists is to try harder at practicing a socially and culturally meaningful archaeology themselves."

People's Need for Authenticity and Inauthenticity

Finally, archaeologists should be aware that not everyone even wants authentic archaeologies—whether scientific or not—and understand what this fact means for professionals who work in the public sphere. An education geared only toward authenticating the past would leave archaeologists ill prepared for interacting with the diverse ways in which people actually use the past. Presenting a correct or genuine account of the past can be of secondary importance to those for whom the past is a conduit to experiences that don't depend on authenticity. Recently, scholars have been especially attuned to the ways that the public uses the past, irrespective of accuracy. Researchers have observed people using material culture and visiting historic sites for a wide variety of reasons that don't necessarily warrant authentic experiences. This, of course, doesn't mean that all inaccuracies are justified or should be judged as equals. It does mean that understanding why the inauthentic exists and how it functions depends on more than just judgments of nominal authenticity.

Sociologist Chris Jenks (1993), in his treatise on cultural reproduction, has argued that selective imitation often has a culturally regenerative role. Creating replicas can be part of an educational or inculcation process that makes the past relevant to the present. But replicas aren't lacking in modern context. Replicas and the act of creating reproductions both perpetuate specific kinds and styles of material culture and make adjustments to suit modern conditions. An example comes from art historian Judith Ostrowitz's (1999) study of the contemporary Native American artists of the U.S.'s and Canada's northwest coast. She has observed these artists using the past in ways similar to an academic's use of citation—not merely as repetition, but as interpretation and selective reference. The artists choose what older styles and forms to incorporate into their work in response to different sets of patrons and different kinds of needs, including the artist's own desires. Ostrowitz notes that items made for outside art buyers are most often hyper-accurate renditions of material culture specifically from the 1800s. Meanwhile, masks and regalia made for contemporary rituals, like potlatches, and public displays inside the local community carry on significant elements of past forms, but they need not conform as closely to only nineteenth-century standards. Both types of work are authentic and inaccurate at the same time, depending on the audience's perspective. Artists are taught—both formally and informally—to follow certain conventions and keep up certain traditions, but they also operate in the contemporary world which demands responses not necessary or even possible in the past. Their work isn't just re-creation. Rather, it is a form of regeneration that keeps their art, and their culture, relevant.

Another example of usage conflicting with accuracy comes from anthropologists Richard Handler and Eric Gable (1996, 1997, 2004). They have spent years studying colonial Williamsburg—a sprawling, open-air reconstruction of the U.S. state of Virginia in the eighteenth century. Colonial Williamsburg is extremely popular—it attracts over a million annual visitors—and has thrived for decades. Here, visitors can tour a replica of the past and learn about the history and use of reconstructed artifacts, buildings, and lifeways. But tourists have been offered much more than just educational experiences over the years. Many people visit places like colonial Williamsburg to shop, eat, physically enjoy themselves, wax nostalgic about a past not nearly as old as the eighteenth century, or to simply get out of the house. Many of these visitors are motivated by forces other than authenticity. They know they might not experience a completely genuine reconstruction of the past, but they appreciate the particulars that the inauthentic version has to offer. Some want to eat a specifically satisfying food or to see a specifically entertaining way of dress in the museum's staff. Some want to experience a particular kind of patriotism. These people are ill served or not even reached by a strictly corrective approach or crusades against inauthentic archaeologies. They aren't engaging the past with an either/or perspective between competing visions of science and pseudoscience. They still want archaeology, but they don't want to choose between competing stories about the past. That's not why they've come.

Kenneth Feder (2002) believes that each generation gets the kind of archaeology it wants, works for, and ultimately deserves. He was advocating for a professionally verified and corrective kind of archaeology when he made this observation. But his point applies as well to inauthentic archaeologies. People—both archaeologists and the general public—turn to archaeology for a wide range of reasons and they don't all want or expect the same. Some ways in which the public uses

More about Colonial Williamsburg

In the mid-1920s, local civic leaders and non-local businessman John D. Rockefeller began a decades-long process of turning the fully functioning, inhabited city of Williamsburg, Virginia, into a massive, open-air tourist attraction. They sought to re-create eighteenth-century America because they believed that first-hand experience with past lifeways would educate visitors about the U.S.'s founding principles of responsible leadership, public service, self-government, and individual liberty. Early American buildings were restored, rebuilt, and re-created in Williamsburg. People—not just docents or reenactors—actually live in the restored town, but the paraphernalia of modern life has been artfully hidden behind the trappings of eighteenth-century architecture. Likewise, scores of docents and guides have been trained to wander the streets in period-specific costumes and interact with the tourists as if they were living in the colonial era. The buildings and streets show what material culture looked like in the past and the guides educate and entertain the site's million-plus annual paying visitors.

Anthropologists Eric Gable and Richard Handler (2004) have noted that, from the attraction's beginning, an ideal of authenticity has had significant influence over how buildings were reconstructed or restored and over what kind of experience is given to the visitors. Colonial Williamsburg's employees began studiously documenting and re-creating the region's historic architecture and material culture at a time in which most historians focused only on texts and archives. They wanted things to appear accurate to the colonial era and aimed for something of a visual authenticity in their re-creations. They were especially successful in this undertaking. Yet, by the second half of the twentieth century, architectural authenticity was no longer sufficient to please either the park's visitors or staff. Things were accurate, but they were like a blueprint rather than a functioning object. They were too perfect. At this point, the whole of colonial Williamsburg was intentionally made dirtier and grittier. Smells, spills, and animal droppings were introduced. Dirt was visible and the site began to reflect the fact that the colonial-era material culture was often broken down, mismatched, or even worn out. Even some of the craftsmen, like the blacksmiths who demonstrated their trade to the tourists and manufactured a variety of souvenirs, were de-skilled to better reflect the times. This was a change in the definition of authenticity. It's not that one period is more authentic than the other because both are re-creations. Each is re-creation at different points in the lifecycles of artifacts and architecture. This hasn't been an easy process nor have the results been entirely satisfying to all of the management and visitors. A dirt-caked past and the spotless ideal of progress are perhaps irreconcilably contrary.

Replication and Regeneration at the Ise Jingu

The Ise Jingu or Ise shrine complex in Japan's Mie Prefecture is another example of a replica having an important role in cultural regeneration. This multi-acre Shinto shrine is one of the most religiously significant in the entire country. It annually hosts many millions of visitors. Pilgrims make their way to the shrine for different reasons and numerous rituals are conducted on site. But Robert Ellwood (1968) explains that the consummate rite at Ise is the Shikinen Sengū. At regular, twenty-year intervals, all two hundred of the wooden buildings of the Inner and Outer shrines are reconstructed next to the originals, which are then torn down. This process has gone on since the first rebuilding in A.D. 620 (the Inner shrine first dates to the third century B.C. and the Outer shrine was originally raised in A.D. 478) and the most recent, sixty-first cycle, culminated in 1993. Each generation of builders use ancient techniques—for instance, carpenters use no nails—to assemble the buildings. Although plans of the site are available, most builders work from direct observation of the last incarnation and the skills of carpentry, metal work, lacquering, and weaving are handed down in long-term apprenticeships. Felicia Bock (1974) observes that the cycle of rebuilding keeps knowledge of these old crafts alive and links each generation of builder and visitor to the last. Her sentiments are shared by Stewart Brand (1999:53), who declares that, "Ise is the world's greatest monument to continuity—an unbroken lineage of structure, records, and tradition on a humid, earthquake-prone, volcanic island." However, the act of re-creating material culture is also one of regeneration in which old ways are continually adjusted for new conditions. For example, Ise became linked to extreme nationalism and imperial conquest in the time prior to World War Two. Yet, Jonathon Reynolds (2001) has shown how, in just a generation, postwar rebuilders were able to neutralize wartime associations and link the site to democratic politics and modernist aesthetic values. They were able to use modernist discourse about local architecture and Watanabe Yoshio's unprecedented and intimate photographs to adjust meanings without disrupting the antiquity of the site or its role as cultural touchstone. Ise Jingu is physically and intellectually both one of the newest and oldest still-functioning structures in the world.

archaeology no doubt appear to archaeologists to be misuses or even abuses of the archaeological record. But we must consider both the legitimate and illegitimate aspects of the inauthentic so we can use inauthenticity as a tool of archaeology without misleading others or ourselves.

How to Use This Book

This book is intended to provide readers with a wide range of examples because inauthenticity is context dependent. The book explores the nuances of archaeology. I wrote it hoping that these examples would serve as fodder for further research. I wrote it so that students of archaeology would compare these examples to what they have encountered in the past as well as what they might come across in the future. Each chapter contrasts with the others and all follow different paths away from a central idea of inauthentic archaeologies. The book is a collection of examples that serve as starting point—it isn't, and shouldn't be, the final word.

Chapter 1 introduces the idea of inauthenticity and establishes some of the terms useful for discussing inauthentic archaeologies. It offers a reason for studying the inauthentic in contrast to the authentic. The chapter highlights the idea that archaeology is context dependent. It also outlines where scholars have taken these ideas in the past as well as where current lines of research are heading.

Chapters 2 and 3 directly address hoaxes, misbegotten science, and frauds. This section starts with perhaps the most well-known and thoroughly discredited hoax in the history of archaeology—Piltdown Man. This examination focuses on why people, including archaeologists, believed in it in the first place and why it took so long to be proven a fraud. Chapter 2 also asks why Piltdown continues to generate so much interest so long after it was exposed. The second chapter in this section explores the fake Anazasi cliff dwellings of Manitou Springs, Colorado, in comparison to more renowned fakes. The cliff dwellings are a popular tourist attraction, but most visitors don't know that Manitou isn't an original site. This chapter examines how professional archaeology interacts with public audiences. It lets us consider what makes some presentations more successful than others and why inauthentic archaeologies might even be more attractive than authentic ones.

Chapter 4 moves the study of inauthentic archaeologies away from just fakes and science versus pseudoscience. It explores the ways in which specific kinds of artifacts come to represent more than themselves and how their meanings might override their origins. The chapter traces the spread of building torreóns (watchtowers) from Spain into the New World. It considers the ways in which modern people use torreóns to constitute culture and how archaeology is reconstituted in advertising, tourism, art, and identity politics.

Chapter 5 looks at archaeology in the service of art in depth. The chapter explicitly recognizes that archaeology serves more than just archaeologists. It offers first-hand insight into why artists have found archaeology to be a particularly fruitful topic with which to engage. Three different artists explain how they perceive professional archaeologists and describe the ways in which artifacts from the past and ideas about prehistory inform their work.

Finally, Chapter 6 examines replica megaliths in Texas. This chapter looks at presentations of archaeology that have no intended educational or didactic message. It explores the physical presence of inauthentic archaeology and considers the role of patently out of place re-creations in people's relationship with the past. It concludes with the idea that sometimes fake archaeology is simply so much fun that questions of accuracy and authenticity do not matter.

A list of references is at the end of each chapter so that readers can explore each example in greater detail and follow bibliographic divergences to even more instances of inauthentic archaeology. The references also provide a context that readers can use to understand more about me—what I've studied, what I've found particularly meaningful, my particular biases, and what might be missing from my perspective. Each chapter also includes a list of critical questions and exercises. These help readers summarize chapters and make connections between them. The questions and exercises help readers compare examples in this book to their own experiences with the archaeological record. Although inauthenticity is context dependent and although this book sets up a discussion about inauthentic versions of the past; nothing can replace first-hand experiences with archaeology. There are many, many inauthentic archaeologies out there, and this book will have served its purpose if the reader goes in search of them.

References and Further Reading

Baudrillard, J.
1994 *Simulacra and Simulation*. Translated by S. F. Glaser. The University of Michigan Press, Ann Arbor.

Benjamin, W.
1969 *Illuminations*. Translated by H. Zohn. Schoken Books, New York.

Bock, F.G.
1974 Rites of Renewal at Ise. *Monumenta Nipponica* 29(1): 55–68.

Brand, S.
1999 *The Clock of the Long Now: Time and Responsibility*. Basic Books, New York.

Cole, J.R., K.L. Feder, F.B. Harrold, R.A. Eve, and A.B. Kehoe
1990 On Folk Archaeology in Anthropological Perspective. *Current Anthropology* 31(4):390–394.

de Boer, T.
2004 *Shovel Bum: Comix of Archaeological Field Life*. AltaMira, Walnut Creek, California.

Dutton, D.
2003 Authenticity in Art. In *The Oxford Handbook of Aesthetics*. J. Levinson, editor. Oxford University Press, New York.

Eco, U.
1986 *Travels in Hyperreality*. Translated by W. Weaver. Harcourt, Brace, Jovanovich, San Diego, California.

Ellwood, R.S.
1968 Harvest and Renewal at the Grand Shrine of Ise. *Numen* 15(3):165–190.

Feder, K.L.
2002 *Frauds, Myths, and Mysteries: Science and Pseudoscience in Archaeology*. McGraw-Hill Mayfield, Boston.

Gable, E. and R. Handler
1996 After Authenticity at an American Heritage Site. *American Anthropologist* 98(3):568–578.

2004 Deep Dirt: Messing up the Past in Colonial Williamsburg. In *Marketing Heritage: Archaeology and the Consumption of the Past*. Y. Rowan and U. Baram, editors. AltaMira, Walnut Creek, California.

Handler, R. and E. Gable
1997 *The New History in an Old Museum: Creating the Past at Colonial Williamsburg.* Duke University Press, Durham, North Carolina.

Holtorf, C.
2005a *From Stonehenge to Las Vegas: Archaeology as Popular Culture.* AltaMira, Walnut Creek, California.
2005b Beyond Crusades: How (Not) to Engage with Alternative Archaeologies. *World Archaeology* 37(4):544–551.

Jenks, C.
1993 *Cultural Reproduction.* Routledge, London.

Kosso, P.
2001 *Knowing the Past: Philosophical Issues of History and Archaeology.* Humanity Books, Amherst, New York.

Lipe, W.D.
2002 Public Benefits of Archaeological Research. In *Public Benefits of Archeology.* B. Little, editor. University Press of Florida, Gainesville.

Michlovic, M.
1990 Folk Archaeology in Anthropological Perspective. *Current Anthropology* 31(1):103–107.
1991 On Archaeology and Folk Archaeology: A Reply. *Current Anthropology* 32(3):321–322.

Ostrowitz, J.
1999 *Privileging the Past: Reconstructing History in Northwest Coast Art.* University of Washington Press, Seattle.

Reynolds, J.M.
2001 Ise Shrine and a Modernist Construction of Japanese Tradition. *The Art Bulletin* 83(2):316–341.

Trigger, B.G.
1989 *A History of Archaeological Thought.* Cambridge University Press, Cambridge.

Williams, S.
1991 *Fantastic Archaeology: The Wild Side of North American Prehistory.* University of Pennsylvania Press, Philadelphia.

Critical Questions and Exercises

1. What reasons might lie behind the fifty-year cut-off date used by the U.S. federal government in most of its archaeological surveys? Specifically consider the reasons offered in this chapter. Do you find any to be more likely or more useful than others? After you make these considerations, do some research. The federal government is very explicit about why it adopted this particular policy, and you can find many discussions of it in government publications available at most libraries and on web pages of federal agencies such as the National Park Service and the Department of the Interior. There is much you determine about the context of the cut-off date. Compare the official explanations with how you expected archaeology to operate.

2. This chapter argues that archaeologists need to be able to communicate effectively with their colleagues in the discipline and the general public. Perform an experiment with the presentation of archaeology. First, try to tell the same story about the archaeological record to at least one archaeologist and one nonarchaeologist. The tale of contemporary flint knapping at Falcon Reservoir or the discussion of the Tübingen-Weilhelm Menhir and the Vasa Warship are good stories to use. Retell the story in your own way, but be especially cognizant of how you choose your words depending on what you expect from each audience. Keep track of the other person's questions and comments. Compare the results of each discussion, including the background details you needed to explain, the listener's interest in the topic, the amount of professional—that is, nonstandard jargon you used, and where the conversation ended.

3. Have you ever visited a museum, archaeology site, or historic reconstruction with the intention of doing something other than learning about the past? Have you ever, like the people who anthropologists Eric Gable and Richard Handler have observed at colonial Williamsburg, gone there to eat, shop, meet people, or just get out of the house? What might this indicate about your own relationship with archaeology and what you expect from presentations of the past?

CHAPTER 2

HOAX AT PILTDOWN

Archaeological frauds and hoaxes are not mistaken ideas or misplaced beliefs about human history. They are explicit attempts to make the past into something for which evidence is unavailable or which available evidence clearly contradicts. The past is such an intriguing and attractive topic of study that many have told outright lies and fabricated physical evidence about it. Some have committed fraud to advance their fundamental beliefs about how the world works, whereas others are motivated by emotions of pride, greed, jealousy, competition, or even the joking joy of making someone else look foolish for believing. Hoaxes can tell us much, through their creation as well as their exposure, about how archaeology operates.

THEY'VE BEEN BRINGING UP FRAGMENTS OF MY SKULL. THESE ARE SMALL, BUT TELLING FRAGMENTS IN UNDERSTANDING WHAT I LOOKED LIKE AND WHAT I DID.

WELL WORN MOLARS

THEY FOUND A BULKY JAW BONE, BUT ITS MOLARS HAD HUMAN LIKE WEAR. THERE WAS ALSO A SINGLE CANINE TOOTH. THIS WAS A VERY SPECIAL SET OF REMAINS BE-CAUSE IT OFFERED DIRECT EVIDENCE AS TO HOW HUMAN EVOL-UTION HAD UNFOLDED.

CANINES

WELL, I'LL BE A MONKEY'S UNCLE!

SCIENTISTS OF THE TIME WERE INTER-ESTED IN "MISSING LINKS" BETWEEN PEOPLE AND THE OTHER PRIMATES.

MY BRAIN SEEMED TO BE ONE KEY TO IT ALL.

33

WE WEREN'T THE FIRST TO DOUBT YOUR EXISTENCE. JUST THE MOST DEFINITIVE!

EVEN EARLY ON THERE WERE THOSE WHO THOUGHT ME TOO PERFECT A FIND — EVEN JOKINGLY SUGGESTING FRAUD!

EACH NEW FIND SINCE MY DISCOVERY SHOWED ME TO BE ANOMALOUS. I WAS ON THE WRONG SIDE OF THE BRAIN VERSUS BODY DEBATE.

SOME LATER RESEARCHERS HAD FOUND PILTDOWN SO OUT OF STEP THAT THEY SIMPLY, QUIETLY LEFT IT OUT OF HYPOTHETICAL FAMILY TREES.

THE FACT THAT I WAS A FRAUD MADE BIG NEWS WORLD-WIDE. THIS WASN'T JUST A BIT OF ACADEMIC INTEREST!

THE COUNTRY OF BRITAIN HAD LOST NATIONAL PRIDE...

ONE OF THE BONE TOOLS HAD EVEN RESEMBLED A BAT USED IN THE PARTICULARLY BRITISH SPORT OF CRICKET!

BRITAIN NO LONGER HOSTED A A KEY LINK IN HUMAN EVOLUTION.

THE QUESTION OF WHO HAD PERPETRATED THE HOAX LOOMED LARGE. PILTDOWN REMAINS INFAMOUS TO THIS DAY NOT JUST BECAUSE THE FRAUD TOOK IN SO MANY FOR SO LONG, BUT BECAUSE THERE ARE SO MANY POSSIBLE SUSPECTS TO CONSIDER...

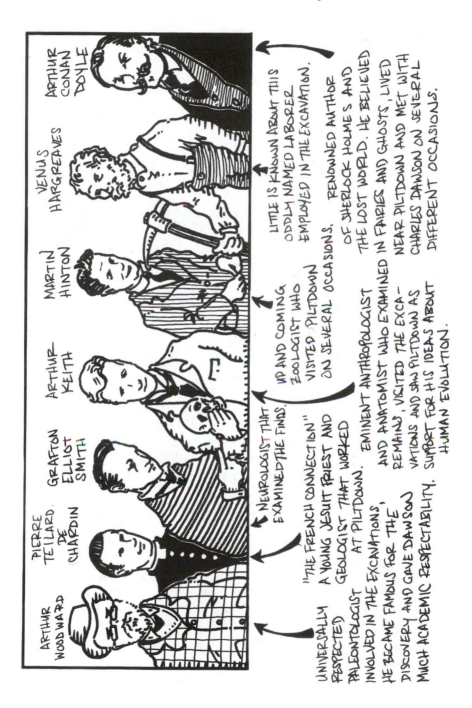

WHY I WAS FAKED IS A VERY MEANINGFUL QUESTION. BUT IT'S ALSO A VERY TENUOUS ONE. SIMPLE ANSWERS AREN'T AS FINAL AS YOU'D EXPECT.

SPECULATING WHY A HOAX WAS PERPETRATED BACK IN 1913 IS JUST AS HARD AS AN ARCHAEOLOGIST PROVING THE PREHISTORIC INTENTIONS THAT LIE BEHIND AN ARTIFACT THAT THEY'VE UNCOVERED.

BASIC HUMAN DRIVES SHOULD GET THE CREDIT.

-REVENGE? -FAME?
-HATRED? -PRIDE?
-RELIGIOUS DOGMA?
-NATIONALISM?
-A JOKE TAKEN TOO FAR?

AUTHOR ALAN MOORE ONCE OBSERVED THAT RESEARCHERS OF JACK THE RIPPER HAD CREATED A SELF-GENERATING, PERPETUAL SERIES OF POSSIBLE PERPETRATORS AND PROBABLE MOTIVES WITH EACH NEW SPECULATION.

I SUSPECT SOMETHING SIMILAR HAS HAPPENED TO ME (WITHOUT THE KNIFE, OF COURSE).

SURE IT WAS DIFFERENT BACK IN OUR DAY. BUT PEOPLE – HUMAN NATURE – HAVEN'T CHANGED ALL THAT MUCH INTO YOUR TIMES.

THE HATS AND MUSTACHES HAVE GONE OUT OF STYLE, BUT THERE ARE STILL FRAUDS COMMITTED (MAYBE NOT AS SPEC-TACULAR, BUT STILL FRAUDS NONETHELESS) AND ARCHAEOLOGISTS CAN STILL SOMETIMES GET THINGS WRONG OR BE FOOLED.

THOSE BASIC, HUMAN MOTIVES ARE STILL AROUND,

-REVENGE? -FAME?
-HATRED? -PRIDE?
-RELIGIOUS DOGMA?
-NATIONALISM?
-A JOKE TAKEN TOO FAR?

TO DENY ARCHAEOLOGISTS THESE MOTIVES IS TO DENY THEM THEIR HUMANITY.

THIS DOESN'T MEAN THAT CREATIONISTS OR EVOLUTION DENIERS ARE RIGHT THOUGH. IT'S THE ALL TOO HUMAN ABILITIES TO BOTH CREATE AND RECOGNIZE PROBLEMS THAT MAKES ARCHAEOLOGY VIBRANT AND VALID. IT'S THE ONLY EFFECTIVE COUN-TER AGAINST DOGMA.

IT WORKS AGAINST THE NARROW MINDED THINKING THAT WOULD'VE NEVER LET US EXPOSE THE HOAX!

THE DISCIPLINE OF ARCHAEOLOGY CAN TAKE CREDIT FOR BEING WRONG, CORRECT ITSELF, AND STILL ADMIT THAT IT'LL BE WRONG AGAIN IN THE FUTURE. THIS IS A POSITIVE THING! IT MEANS ARCHAEOLOGY STILL HAS MUCH TO OFFER.

DIGGING THROUGH THE PAST - EVEN IF IT'S THEIR OWN PAST - IS PART OF THE ARCHAEOLOGIST'S JOB DESCRIPTION. THEY HAVE SOME POWERFUL TOOLS AT THEIR DISPOSAL AND GOOD THINGS - LIKE EXPOSING HOAXES - HAPPEN WHEN THEY USE THEM.

HOAXES AND FRAUDS WILL BE PERPETRATED. BUT ARCHAEOLOGISTS WILL CONTINUE DIGGING - THROUGH BOTH THE PREHISTORIC PAST AND THEIR OWN HISTORY.

• REFERENCES AND FURTHER READING •

- C. CHIPPINDALE (1991) PILTDOWN: WHO DUNIT? WHO CARES? SCIENCE. 250(39):1162-1163
- N. CLERMONT (1992) ON THE PILTDOWN JOKER AND ACCOMPLICE: A FRENCH CONNECTION? CURRENT ANTHROPOLOGY. 33(5):587-589
- S.J. GOULD (1983) HEN'S TEETH AND HORSE'S TOES. NORTON, NEW YORK, NEW YORK
- A. MOORE AND E. CAMPBELL (1999) FROM HELL. EDDIE CAMPBELL COMICS, PADDINGTON, AUSTRALIA
- P.V. TOBAIS (1992) PILTDOWN: AN APPRAISAL OF THE CASE AGAINST SIR ARTHUR KEITH. CURRENT ANTHROPOLOGY. 33(3):243-293
- J.E. WALSH (1996) UNRAVELING PILTDOWN. RANDOM HOUSE, NEW YORK, NEW YORK
- J.S. WEINER (1955) THE PILTDOWN FORGERY. OXFORD, LONDON, ENGLAND
- A.S. WOODWARD (1948) THE EARLIEST ENGLISHMAN. WATTS, LONDON, ENGLAND.

WORDS & PICTURES
TROY R. LOVATA '06

Shinichi Fujimura and the Faking of the Japanese Paleolithic

The Piltdown hoax was especially egregious. But it was less unique than many people might expect or hope. Another massive archaeological fraud came to light nearly a half century after Kenneth Oakley, Joseph Wiener, and Wilfrid Le Gros Clark definitively exposed Piltdown. Archaeologist Shoh Yamada (2002) recounts that in the early morning of October 22, 2000, reporters from the Mainichi Shinbun newspaper videotaped renowned archaeologist Shinichi Fujimura planting artifacts at the Japanese Paleolithic site of Kamitakamori. Within months, the paper printed photographs of him salting the excavation. Fujimura admitted the fraud on television and retired to a psychiatric hospital, a decades-long career was under suspicion, and the whole idea of a Japanese Paleolithic era began to crumble.

Shinichi Fujimura had become an academic and media darling over the previous two decades for helping push back the earliest evidence of human settlement in Japan from 35,000 to 600,000 years before the present. He was easily the most respected amateur archaeologist in Japan—where amateurs and professionals often work together—and benefited from an amiable relationship with respected Professor Chosuke Serizawa of Tohoku University. Shinichi Fujimura's 1981 discovery of the then oldest find in Japan jump-started a career that included: work on 180 different sites, an honored place in the Japanese Archaeological Association, a position as the deputy director of the Tohoku Paleolithic Institute, special mention in the nation's textbooks, and the nickname "God's Hand" for his uncanny ability to uncover artifacts that repeatedly dated older than the last. A few archaeologists, such as Shizuo Oda and Charles Keally (1986), had expressed doubts about the veracity of many of Fujimura's previous finds. They were basically ignored. Moreover, finds were often isolated and lacking in associated materials, such as animal remains, that could support the increasingly older dates. But this was explained away as being due to soil conditions. Most academics failed to notice or take the inconsistencies seriously. In the end, it was the same

Critical Questions and Exercises

1. Although the Piltdown Man was discredited long ago, it is important to understand the continuing presence of this particular hoax in both academic and popular culture. How many people have been attracted by the story and the supposed mystery of who did it? You should do some literary research—count how many books and articles you can find about Piltdown. Can you identify more than a hundred references? More than five hundred? What does the length and kind public attention that aided the ascendancy of both Fujimura and Japanese Paleolithic research—and that some say stifled any real criticism—that led to his and its downfall.

An investigation by the Japanese Archaeological Association eventually concluded that Shinichi Fujimura had planted evidence not just at Kamita-kamori, but at over 150 different archaeology sites. Many of the artifacts he had uncovered were shown to be authentic pieces taken from much younger sites. The whole concept of a Japanese Paleolithic was thrown into disarray because Fujimura and his many finds were central to defining the era. Japan's human habitation has basically been reset at less than 35,000 years ago. This is something of a national disgrace. It also helps explain—although not entirely—why many people believed in the finds or, at least, failed to criticize them when they did have doubts. Evidence for an increasingly older Paleolithic period had been celebrated for supporting ethnic and national unique-ness and countering evidence that the islands had been settled by people from the Korean Peninsula. Shinichi Fujimura's personal motivations aren't entirely clear. He admitted to some, but not all, of the incidences of fraud. Yamada (2002:48) gave the bizarre explanation that "the devil made me do it" and even claimed to have multiple personalities. Some have blamed the stress of being both an archaeology and media star and the push to uncover yet another impressive find. Shoh Yamada (2002:54) notes that there has been constructive criticism in the speculation, but that:

> some less informed critics have used the scandal as a platform for sen-sationalism and self-aggrandizement. Criticism from abroad—some well-deserved, and some poorly informed and opportunistic—has been particularly stinging. Finally, the continuing mystery surrounding the case has bred rampant speculation, with some people even suggesting the existence of as-yet-unrevealed collaborators.

of citations on your list tell you about the impact and enduring pres-ence of Piltdown?

2. Piltdown Man himself certainly hasn't stood the test of time. However, it's worth asking if the motives behind this hoax still drive people in the twenty-first century. This chapter argues that basic human drives were not only at work in both creating and exposing the fraud, but also lend archaeology a necessary vibrancy. First, explore your personal perspective. Make a list of the fundamental drives that carry you through an average week. Then consider how the things that motivate you might impact your role as an archaeologist. Are you competitive or cooperative? Are you patriotic? Do you think of yourself as traditional or alternative? Do you believe what most people tell you or are you fundamentally suspicious? Remember to consider both positive and negative impacts of what motivates you.

Second, compare Piltdown to Shinichi Fujimura's recent faking of numerous of Japanese Paleolithic artifacts and sites. He seems to share motivations with suspects like Charles Dawson—including seeking respect, personal glory, and national pride. His conclusions about the past, like those made about Piltdown, were the kind of answers that many had wanted to believe. Finally, Shinichi's fakes were also shown to be a big story that fell apart in the details—such as improper discoloration of artifacts in contrast to their supposed age and the resemblance of his finds to artifacts from later time periods. Specifically compare and contrast the two sets of hoaxes. Are the motivations for someone to create a hoax and the reasons for others to believe in it still valid three-quarters of a century later?

3. Piltdown Man was exposed as a hoax because of incongruent details. When taken as a whole, the Piltdown finds seemed to provide a complete answer to a significant question of human evolution. Yet the sheer number of inconsistencies between the separate artifacts couldn't stand up to the intense scrutiny that was finally applied in the 1950s. Nevertheless, small details also seem to have a role in keeping alive the seemingly endless speculation about the perpetrator or perpetrators. Examinations of minor details—like the casual relationships between people, the places people traveled to before and after the initial discovery, the times that individuals are unaccounted for, brief mentions of people in Arthur Conan Doyle's books, and the fact that some involved in the dig or analysis were especially close friends or truly disliked each other—appear to have greatly increased the number of suspects and the possible reasons for creating such a significant fake. That Charles Dawson is the most likely culprit is tempered by all the possible perpetrators brought up when considering these other facts. Examine this paradox of details. Consider how it affects our ability to know how hoaxes function and how they affect the discipline of archaeology.

CHAPTER 3

THE FAKE ANASAZI OF MANITOU SPRINGS

It is often hard to differentiate between authentic archaeology, what's been re-created, and what is fantastical. It's worthwhile to ask if someone can distinguish them just by looking. Yet, even being able to identify an inauthentic artifact doesn't mean you know the complicated process through which it came into being. Simply labeling something inauthentic is akin to having an authentic artifact about which you know nothing of the contexts of manufacture, use, discard, or discovery. There are important stories behind what looks real, what doesn't, and why.

Archaeology and Tourism in the Southwest

The state of Colorado is bisected north to south by mountains. Here the flatness of Great Plains meets the steepness of the Rocky Mountains and the tree-covered Rockies then taper into the Southwest desert. This jumble of physiographic zones is matched by many, many years of different peoples moving into the region from different directions and for distinctly different reasons. Big-game hunting Paleoindians, sedentary farming peoples, nomads on foot and on horseback, successive groups recognized as modern Native Americans, and settlers with roots in many different parts of Europe have all made this place home at one time or another. Even today, this region has one of the fastest-growing populations in the country. Metropolitan areas like Denver and Colorado Springs have attracted recent settlement as much because of the mountain vistas and outdoor lifestyle as economic development and the promise of jobs. The cultural and natural qualities that bring flocks of tourists to the area are the same that have convinced many to stay. In fact, tourism has been a foundation of both Colorado's economy and sense of cultural self for over a century.

49

The small town of Manitou Springs, situated just above Colorado Springs proper, is a prime example of the role of tourism in the state. European American settlement at the base of the 14,110 foot Pike's Peak waned and waxed through the mid- to late-1800s as ranching and mining variously boomed and busted. But by the turn of the twentieth century, Manitou Springs had fashioned itself into a tourist town of the healthy, friendly, and quaint variety. It used its hot springs and location as a stepping-off point into the mountain wilderness to build a relatively sustainable economy of tourism. The pleasures and pursuits of the visitors have shifted and changed over time, but Manitou Springs has found ways to meet and shape their demands. Today, the town continues to serve as a gateway to outdoor activities—the roads, hiking trails, and cog-wheel railroad up Pike's Peak start here, and the geological attractions of the Garden of the Gods, the Cave of the Winds, and Royal Gorge are all nearby. An active chamber of commerce is also quick to point out that Manitou Springs hosts a variety of cultural attractions like the preserved Victorian elegance of Miramont Castle. The town is also part of the thoroughly modern Southwest and thus caters to a fairly sizable New Age community looking for spiritual connections in people as well as place. Even the area's namesake natural springs have garnered renewed interest for their healthful, if not healing, properties. One of the most popular of the area's attractions has long been the cliff dwellings in Phantom Canyon. They are a well-advertised and well-attended tourist stop. A hundred years worth of visitors have come here for the opportunity to wander through stone room blocks tucked under the cliffs. They come to watch Native American dancers, to learn about the archaeological remains of the mysterious Anasazi culture, and, of course, to purchase souvenirs.

The single set of cliff dwellings at Manitou Springs are less monumentally imposing than the sprawling and much better known sites of Chaco Canyon and Mesa Verde (which lie several hundred miles to the southwest). However, this place is clearly related to other Anasazi sites big and small. The Anasazi and the remnants of their culture are fairly well defined in both the public consciousness and the typologies of academic researchers. Compact apartments of stone block, black-on-white pottery, a sedentary lifestyle, a conservative religion that permeated the community, and corn agriculture are seen as hallmarks of the Anasazi. This group is recognized as ancestral to many

Figure 3.1 Entering the Manitou Springs Cliff Dwellings

Visitors encounter a story of the Anasazi as soon as they pay their admission and enter the parking lot. The cliff dwellings themselves are in full view and flanked by meaning. To the right, a tipi in Plains Indian style is meant to contrast a common view of nomadic Native Americans against more permanent habitations and life-styles. To the left is a snack bar built in the style of Taos Pueblo. It is meant to show links between the Anasazi and Puebloan peoples currently living in the Southwest.

Figure 3.2 A Typical Anasazi Home

The cliff dwellings are constructed in what most people think of as a traditional Anasazi style. They are multiple-story stone dwellings with wood beams—known as vigas—supporting the upper floors. Wooden ladders and balconies connect small, rectangular, and t-shaped windows and doors. The long benches in the center, foreground of this picture, are spectator seating for the daily Native American dance demonstrations.

of the modern Puebloan peoples of the Four Corners region (that area radiating from the junction of the states of Arizona, Utah, Colorado, and New Mexico), but they have also long been associated with a general view of the American Southwest as an ancient and mysterious region.

The very look of the Manitou cliff dwellings lets learned expert and casual tourist alike know that this place is Anasazi. The curl of a large rock overhang rises above one side of a wide canyon and defines and protects an interconnected series of multi-story, stone structures (figure 3.1). Sets of wooden ladders and short balconies connect distinctive and dainty rectangular and t-shaped windows and doorways. These allow entrance into small, squared rooms that housed the daily lives of prehistoric peoples (figure 3.2). A diminutive, circular kiva can be found in the depths of the cliff dwelling.

Figure 3.3 Museum Displays

A building in the style of Taos Pueblo, a still-occupied Native American settlement in New Mexico, was built next to the cliff dwellings. Until the mid-1980s, this building was the home of the Native Americans who danced at Manitou. Today, it contains a large gift shop and a small museum. The museum's displays are primarily glass cases filled with artifacts and dioramas that illustrate different aspects of Anasazi life.

This semi-subterranean room with a hearth and sacred *sipapu* (a hole through which people emerged into the current world) intimates the social and spiritual underpinnings of the Anasazi world. Throughout the site, exposed *vigas*, beams, and breaks in the masonry reveal ancient construction techniques. The site appears to be eroding and this seems to set its construction well back in antiquity.

But it's not just the prehistoric-looking features that let visitors know that this is an ancient and Anasazi place. The cliff dwellings are clearly surrounded by all the trappings of a museum. Well-marked signage leads tourists and welcomes busloads of school groups to a paved parking lot just steps from the site itself. Visitors make their way inside the cliff dwelling and there they find plaques explaining the different uses of each room. Areas directly adjacent to the stone structures have been set aside for frequent Native American dances. A globular, horno-style oven is on hand for demonstrations of traditional cooking methods. Scattered about the grounds are even more signs that identify native plants and explain their customary—medicinal, nutritional, recreational—uses. A Plains Indian tipi and a building in the style of Taos Pueblo have been constructed nearby to help explain the links and differences with other Native peoples. These structures also situate the Anasazi firmly within a larger picture of American prehistory. The Pueblo-style building houses a modest series of glass cases that display Anasazi farming tools, pottery artifacts, and dioramas of past lifeways (figure 3.3). Finally, a patio snack bar and extensive gift shop are nearby. All the things that signify a certifiable cultural attraction seem to be here.

However, apart from its familiar look, the Manitou cliff dwellings are different from other local and regional archaeology attractions. Many people, including archaeologists like Caryn Berg (2002), find it surprising that the site is privately owned. This isn't widely advertised, but when asked, the owners freely admit that they are a money-making business. This is clearly in contrast to many of the best-known sites and museums in the region. Massive archaeology sites like Mesa Verde and Chaco Canyon have been deemed significant enough parts of the national patrimony that they are federally owned and controlled as national parks. Other sites and collections of artifacts in the region, like the Museum of Natural History at the University of Colorado, are state or municipal supported. Finally, some private archaeology centers, like the well-regarded Crow Canyon Archaeology Center, are nonprofits that enjoy a governmentally recognized tax exempt status. Ownership and profit motive are important when considering the context of archaeology. They can help visitors understand why particular items are on display and why certain artifacts have been deemed worthy of preservation. But, at the same time, the Manitou cliff dwellings are by no means the only privately owned archaeology site or for-profit museum in the American Southwest. Many people fail to realize that much of U.S. archaeology is actually privately owned. Laws declare that most artifacts found on private land are private property. Even many of America's national parks were purchased from, or donated by, private owners. The cliff dwellings at Manitou Springs are but one of thousands of sites located on private land and one of many museums operated for profit.

But the Manitou cliff dwellings are different from attractions like Mesa Verde or Chaco Canyon for reasons beside ownership and profit. The Manitou cliff dwellings are different because they are fake.

The Anasazi, Faked

Manitou Springs lies far outside the widely accepted boundaries of Anasazi settlement, which centered around the San Juan River basin in the Four Corners area of Colorado (see, for instance, Linda Cordell 1984, 1994). The cliff dwellings themselves were built about a hundred years ago—between A.D. 1896 and 1906. This is long after the fourteenth century A.D. date that most archaeologists identify as the transition point from the Anasazi to modern Puebloan peoples. The masonry used to construct the dwellings is real enough. Much of the site is built of stones taken from a set of collapsed Anasazi ruins in the southwestern corner of Colorado. So the rocks themselves are authentic enough. Yet, prior to the turn of the last century, a cliff dwelling never existed in Phantom Canyon. There was perhaps never a more aptly named geographic feature in which to encounter such a site.

The cliff dwellings aren't the only fake cultural attraction in the area. The Christmas-themed Santa's Workshop and North Pole lies just up the road from Manitou Springs at a decidedly nonpolar 38 degrees north latitude. But few adults visit there believing in Santa Claus. The Manitou cliff dwellings are significant because they represent the Anasazi in specifically museum and educational contexts. They are meant to be explanatory. Visitors to Manitou believe in the

Anasazi, believe in what they represent, and believe the stories told about them. Scholars like Robert Ellis (1997) and Eric Gary Anderson (1999) note that the Anasazi and their Puebloan descendants play an important role in how America defines itself. They give it depth of time, add particular shape to its architecture, and diversify its way of life. The very idea of the Anasazi is powerful enough that someone has faked a set of their ruins. How their story is presented and who does the presentation exposes the processes by which we describe and subsequently redefine the past. The story of the Anasazi is so influential and attractive that control of it is a valuable thing. The Manitou cliff dwellings show how professional study, scholarly presentation, and public understanding of the past interact. Both powerful and lesser-known figures in American archaeology were intimately involved in its construction and gave it their approval. These fake structures bring up questions of authenticity and authority. They force visitors to consider why they believe in particular stories of the past and force scholars to consider their role as the arbiters of prehistory.

Archaeologists' Responsibilities and Artifacts' Value

Professional archaeologists usually react strongly when faced with fake artifacts or sites. We are particularly attuned to our responsibilities to protect, preserve, and promote an understanding of the past. The concept that the past is a public resource held in professional trust is deeply enshrined in the codes of conduct of groups like the Society for American Archaeology. Most archaeology textbooks, which are key in training future generations of scholars, highlight these responsibilities. Archaeologists continually question where work rises from, reconsider evidence, and consider what is hypothesis as opposed to fact. Archaeology is the study of real people. Therefore, professional scholars rarely face a disinterested public because everyone has some connection—at least legally, if not emotionally—to the past. William Lipe (2002) explains that because archaeologists attempt to produce credible accounts of what happened in the past, we have a responsibility to authenticate not just theories about past peoples and events, but the artifacts themselves. Diane Barthel's (1996) examination of the historical preservation movement shows that physical artifacts hold special value for those studying the past. Their very tangibility separates them from historic texts or media representations and they deserve to be treated with extra care. The combination of an archaeologist's responsibilities and an artifact's value equal an enormous interest in the authentic. Most archaeologists think that only real evidence can produce real understanding. Lipe (2002) explains that various restorations, reproductions, and virtual representations can be effective ways to help the public "connect" with the past if a proper context is given. But most archaeologists cringe at the unlabeled fake.

In fact, Manitou Springs' visitors are given few indications that the cliff dwellings are fake. There are certainly no obvious signs explaining the fakery the way that plaques scattered about the place

Florida's Holy Land Experience

The construction of out-of-place archaeology sites as tourist attractions wasn't just an early twentieth-century phenomenon. In February 2001, Marvin Rosenthal's evangelical, Protestant Christian ministry opened the Holy Land Experience just a few miles south of Orlando, Florida. Archaeologist Yorke Rowan (2004) has conducted an extensive examination of this modern American replica of parts of Israel, Palestine, and Jordan between 1450 B.C. and A.D. 70. His survey of this fifteen-acre, $16-million biblical theme park offers an interesting comparison to the cliff dwellings at Manitou Springs. Professor Rowan (2004:257–259) notes that there is a history of Holy Land replica's in America, including Palestine Park in New York built in the late-1800s as part of the Chautauqua religious movement and a re-creation of Jerusalem at the 1904 World's Fair in St. Louis, Missouri. These were built to offer visitors immersive, hands-on educational experiences. The Holy Land Experience, as seen through both promotional literature and first-hand observation, purports to give its visitors the same.

The Holy Land Experience, like the Manitou cliff dwellings, offers the chance to wander through period-specific buildings and landscapes and interact with the occasional employee performing rituals in ancient looking—cowl and sandal—garb. Tourists enter through turnstiles located in a replica of the Jaffa Gate of the Old City of Jerusalem. Then, after passing through the Jerusalem Street Market, they can stop at the Wilderness Tabernacle (modeled after a Bedouin tent) or cross a plaza lined with Roman columns to the Temple of the Great King (a six-story building based on the façade of the Herodian Temple). Nearby, the Via Dolorosa leads past a Roman road and Middle Eastern plants to the Calvary's Garden Tomb. This unembellished tomb cut into stone represents the place outside Jerusalem that Protestants consider to be the site of Jesus Christ's burial and resurrection (the Catholic and Orthodox churches mark another site—not represented at the Holy Land Experience—as the place of Christ's entombment).

offer insight into Anasazi archaeology. The architecture, apart from the Plains Indian tipi and museum/gift shop/snack bar in the style of Taos Pueblo, is labeled as Anasazi. Archaeologists in other times and places have used methods to distinguish between the real and reconstructed, such as the use of distinctly colored, obviously modern, or stylistic neutral materials to fill in the cracks and around out the missing sections. But these are absent at Manitou Springs. Even the brochure given to each admission-paying visitor walks the finest of semiotic lines by noting that these authentic cliff dwellings were first opened to the public in 1907. Only those who purchase the extra

Other attractions include a re-creation of the Qumran Dead Sea Cave, the Shofar Auditorium, which houses a scale model of the entire city of Jerusalem in A.D. 66, and the Scriptorium—home to a collection of authentic ancient scrolls. Finally, a cafeteria offers up semi-fast food and gift shops throughout the site give visitors ample opportunity to purchase an especially wide range of souvenirs.

There are more, and more organized, interactive events at the Holy Land Experience than at the Manitou Cliff Dwellings Museum. Moreover, the larger number of period-dressed performers in these presentations are not advertised as direct descendents of Semitic peoples like the Native American dancers at Manitou Springs. This indicates a notable difference between the two parks. Authenticity at the Holy Land Experience is based more on an appeal to spiritual accuracy rather than claims of material originality. Visitors know that they aren't in the Holy Lands and aren't viewing, apart from the artifacts in the Scriptorium, original material culture. The places and events portrayed at the park are explicitly Christian and visitors come for a biblically, rather than archaeologically, accurate experience. Stories derived from archaeology and the display of ancient material culture are still meaningful—especially when they are used to argue biblical views of the past—but the site's function doesn't depend on them. Yorke Rowan (2004:263) explains that:

> The distance from the authentic place located within Israel/Palestine is not of vital concern to visitors attracted to the [Holy Land Experience], because people are interested in constructing authentic relationships with a particular retelling of the past, and that past assists in the construction or reaffirmation in a sense of identity.

First and foremost, visitors come to the Holy Land Experience to strengthen their religious beliefs.

$1.29 museum guide are informed that it was likely that the Anasazi never tread on Phantom Canyon soil and that the site is described as authentic only because the stones did, in fact, come from an actual Anasazi dwelling in another part of the state. Archaeologist Robert Leonard (1999) notes that during his visit to the site, neither the tourists, the gift shop personnel, nor the museum guides seemed to understand the fakery at hand.

A Fake's History and Archaeology's Involvement

Over the last one hundred years, many different archaeologists have voiced their opposition to what the Manitou cliff dwellings appear to stand for and how the site operates (for example, see Berg 2002, Smith 2002). It is understandable that professional archaeologists might disdain this place, especially in comparison to clearly labeled re-creations and reconstructions. It seems to be an affront to what the discipline of archaeology is supposed to stand for. It is easy to imagine professionals taking on an "us versus them" mindset when visiting Manitou Springs. This has happened before when archaeologists have faced things like creationists, pseudo-scientists, and the acts of gods used to explain human endeavors. But there's a problem with such strong views. They tend to gloss over important and subtle distinctions about what occurs between the tourist and the story presented. They essentially, prematurely, end any discussion about the power of stories about the past. Such positions ignore the fact there is no "them" to be versus because professional, even respected, archaeologists are central to the Manitou cliff dwelling's very existence.

A fake archaeology site doesn't merely exist in place, waiting to be discovered or uncovered. A fake archaeology site needs to be brought into existence with hard work, perseverance, and money. It takes a tremendous amount of effort to move several tons of rock over three hundred miles, assemble replicas of the Spruce Tree House and Cliff Palace structures at Mesa Verde National Park, and convince people to visit. The story of the Anasazi is important enough that someone has found it worth the hard work of faking.

At its heart, the Manitou cliff dwellings are a product of the momentous late- and early-twentieth-century struggle to define and professionalize archaeology in the Southwest. These were formative years. They defined not only the typologies of artifacts and cultural histories archaeologists continue to use today, but also influenced how archaeological research is carried out. There were many archaeologists who rose to prominence during this period. One of the most important was Dr. Edgar Lee Hewett.

Dr. Hewett was crucial in shaping southwestern and, by extension, U.S. archaeology into its present configuration. Hewett was president of New Mexico Highlands University and professor of anthropology at the University of New Mexico and San Diego State Teachers College. He founded the Departments of Anthropology at the University of New Mexico, the University of Southern California, and San Diego State University. He founded the School of American Research, the Museum of New Mexico and the Indian Market in Santa Fe. He personally shaped the centerpiece of federal archaeological protection legislation—the 1906 Antiquities Act. He also enlisted the help and support of numerous volunteers and amateur archaeologists in preserving America's past. American archaeology, as both an academic discipline and a public attraction, with all its advances and problems alike, would not exist without the presence of Edgar Lee Hewett at the turn of the last century.

Hewett was a westerner at heart and a stubborn defender of the causes he believed in. He was nicknamed "El Toro" (the bull) and he, along with many others in the region, fought a long-running battle to wrest control of archaeology in the Southwest from the eastern establishment of the Archaeological Institute of America, the Smithsonian Institution, and Harvard and Columbia Universities. This was both a political and an academic struggle and, of course, it entailed more than just Hewett himself. This was a regional struggle. It touched on who was allowed to excavate, where artifacts were studied and housed, how parks would set up to protect archaeological resources, and how resource protection legislation was to be crafted. Battles were fought back and forth within the halls of academia, on the pages of newspapers and popular magazines, and during legislative sessions.

Archaeologists and historians like Joseph Weixelman (2004), Duane Smith (2002), Don Fowler (2000), and Linda Cordell (1994) have outlined how a particularly significant struggle took place for control and exhibition of the Southwest's Anasazi archaeology. At the beginning of the twentieth century, the idea of the Anasazi was gaining national prominence. The World's Columbian Exposition, held in Chicago in 1893, included specific collections of Anasazi artifacts from

Mesa Verde in Colorado. At the time, world expositions and fairs had a nearly unmatched ability to shape public opinion and set the tone of intellectual discussion. The Anasazi artifacts on display in Chicago were collected by a Colorado rancher named Richard Wetherill who, just five years before the exposition, had stumbled onto Mesa Verde's especially well-preserved and extensive ruins. Wetherill brought a young Swedish archaeologist named Baron Gustaf Nordenskjold to the site in 1891. Ten years later, Baron Nordenskjold published the first academic study of Mesa Verde, and professional interest in the Anasazi matched growing public attention. The idea of the Anasazi was quickly becoming an important part of both the American consciousness and the self-definition of southwestern states. The black-on-white pottery, the masonry house blocks, and the names of specific sites were on the minds of an increasing number of people.

Sites like Mesa Verde began attracting more and more tourists in the years following the 1893 exhibition. They also attracted people with interests in studying, preserving, protecting, and displaying Anasazi archaeology. Interest rose to such a level that between 1901 and 1905 several federal bills were put forward to create a Colorado Cliff Dwellings Park—later known as Mesa Verde National Park—based around an especially extensive and well-preserved series of Anasazi sites. A battle ensued over control of these archaeological sites as either federal or state-run entities. The question of who would control Mesa Verde didn't just concern preserving important pieces of the archaeological record. It affected how tourists would visit the sites and who would profit from their tours. It would affect the direction of future economic growth in the region and how people would be able to use the past as cultural currency.

Of course, "El Toro" Hewett was involved in this struggle, but another key figure was a compatriot of Hewett's named Virginia McClurg. She headed the prominent and powerful (and, interestingly enough, all female-run) Colorado Cliff Dwellings Association. The association had been formed to foster knowledge of Anasazi sites in the state and acted as a self-appointed advocate for prehistory. Historian Duane Smith (2002) has described McClurg and her associates as "Women to the Rescue" who successfully lobbied for the preservation of much Colorado archaeology. In the end, McClurg and the association were successful in promoting cliff dwellings, but not in keeping them under local jurisdiction. The creation of Mesa Verde

National Park in 1906 eventually cemented federal control of many significant Anasazi sites.

Virginia McClurg had done much to promote Colorado's archaeology, but she was embittered by the solidification of federal control. She wanted sites preserved, protected, and available for tourists, but, like Hewett, she also wanted them firmly under regional management and local jurisdiction. In response to Mesa Verde becoming a national park, McClurg threw her support behind a plan to build a set of Anasazi cliff dwellings in Manitou Springs. The citizens of Manitou Springs had joined with Harold Ashenhurst, of the Ashenhurst Amusement Company, in a bid to capture some of the tourist trade heading for Mesa Verde. They proposed the building, or perhaps rebuilding, of a set of cliff dwelling in the area.

Manitou Springs was well situated for tourists. It was located along the Front Range and was more accessible to trains (and later cars and buses) than Colorado's far southwestern corner. McClurg's endorsement of the project caused a major rift in the Colorado Cliff Dwellings Association. Members from the Durango area quit in protest, but she and the site persisted. At some point, it appears that Hewett, who was arbiter of all southwestern archaeology and shared McClurg's sense of western self-determination, gave the site his approval. Historian Joseph Weixelman (2004) has found letters from Hewett actually disparaging the Manitou Springs cliff dwellings, but his role as a consultant in its construction is noted by those who run the Manitou cliff dwellings and archaeologist Robert Leonard found his picture proudly displayed when he visited in 1999.

Authority and Public Perception

Professional archaeology had a hand, both directly and indirectly, in shaping the Manitou Springs cliff dwellings. This exposes an interesting process of public and professional interaction. It highlights how people act as authorities about the past as well as the differences between how the discipline of archaeology presents itself and how it is received.

Although Virginia McClurg and Edgar Lee Hewett were entwined with the Manitou cliff dwellings, it is important to remember that their methods and beliefs were a product of the time. Archaeologists today, like most other professions, operate in manners quite different

Giants in New York and Vikings in Minnesota

Harold Ashenhurst and the citizens of Manitou Springs weren't the first to come up with the idea of using inauthentic archaeology as a tourist attraction and small-town economic engine. Archaeologist Kenneth Feder recounts the story of the Cardiff Giant in his popular book *Frauds, Myths, and Mysteries: Science and Pseudoscience in Archaeology* (2002). What appeared to be a fossil of an ancient, giant man was discovered by farmer Stub Newell in 1869 near the town of Cardiff in upstate New York. A "Giant Mania" ensued, the tourists poured in, and Newell himself gave up farming to exhibit the find full time. Eventually, the tourist onslaught outstripped the resources of tiny Cardiff and nearby Syracuse took up the slack. Feder (2002:48) notes that, "the economic impact of the Giant on Syracuse cannot be underestimated and was enough to convince a consortium of Syracuse businessmen and professional people to make Stub an offer he couldn't refuse." They purchased a three-quarter share of the find for what would be more than a million dollars by today's standards. The Cardiff Giant was soon shown to be a hoax crafted by Newell and his relatives to affirm the biblical story of David and Goliath. Yet its economic impact didn't end with it being thoroughly exposed as a fake. The giant was eventually purchased by the New York State Historical Society in 1947 and installed in the Cooperstown Farmer's Museum, where people—including Feder himself—still pay for the opportunity to behold it.

But the outlay of Syracuse's businessmen pales in comparison to the investment that local leaders, several different towns, and the state of Minnesota have made over the last century in promoting the Kensington Runestone. Archaeologist Michael Michlovic (1990, 1991) has conducted an in-depth study of this two-hundred-pound rock and the cultural impact it's had since its discovery in 1898. The Runestone was purportedly found entangled in the roots of a tree by Swedish immigrant Olaf Ohman in the small town of Kensington, Minnesota. The rock is supposedly inscribed with the story of fourteenth-century Scandinavian, also known as Norse or Viking, explorers who met an untimely death in the area—presumably at the hands of Native Americans. Research at L'Anse aux Meadows in Newfoundland, Canada, has proven that Vikings had reached and shortly settled in the New World some five hundred years before Christopher Columbus in 1492. But Michael Michlovic notes that there is little conclusive evidence of Vikings in the Upper Midwest and that most academics identify the Kensington Runestone as a fake. Nevertheless, many Minnesotans continue to afford the rock a special status and believe in the authenticity of both it and Viking settlement in the region. Over two million Scandinavians immigrated to North America between 1850 and 1930 and vast numbers settled in the upper Midwest. Archaeologist Michlovic attributes their faith and interest in the stone and associated Viking exploration to the process of cultural integration into American society. The massive numbers of immigrants and their descendants used and continue to use the past to both highlight their unique ethnicity and construct a meaningful history for themselves within the national tapestry. Outside the Douglas County Museum in Alexandria, Minnesota—where the Kensington Runestone is on permanent display— stands a colorful, larger-than-life statue of an armor-clad Viking warrior. "Big Ole" holds a spear in one hand and a shield in the other. Writing on the shield is visible from quite a distance and reads, "Alexandria, Birthplace of America."

Olaf Ohman sold the Kensington Runestone to private researcher Hjalmar Holand in 1907. Holand etched a letter "H" into the rock and took it on an extensive tour that included a 1948 exhibition at the Smithsonian Institution in Washington, D.C. The rock formed the basis for a lifetime of Holand's lectures, research articles, and books (including Holand 1910, 1932, 1935, 1946, 1962). But Holand's purchase was only the first of many investments into the Runestone's fame. The museum in Alexandria attracts thousands of paying visitors each year. Michlovic (1990:105) observes that the sign over its entrance reads "'Alexandria Chamber of Commerce— Runestone Museum—Tourist Information—Douglas County Historical Society—Alexandria Development Corp.' and reflects the close association between a version of the past and local business interests." Nearby Kensington has also put money into promoting and celebrating the find. The municipality landscaped a park with pavilions around the discovery site, paved roads through the park, and erected several prominent monuments to mark the event. Michlovic (1990:105) explains that, "one of these monuments lists the contributors to the construction of the park, which includes public utilities, service clubs, public organizations and churches—virtually every public institution in the Kensington community." Even the town's Catholic Church is even named "Our Lady of the Runestone." The local bishop reasoned that it didn't really matter if the stone was authentic or not. It was still the biggest event ever in the town's history and warranted the honor. Finally, Michlovic explains that the tale of the Kensington Runestone produced perhaps an even bigger economic spin-off in the resort community of Val Chatel. In the summers of 1986 and 1987, the resort staged a spectacular outdoor drama, entitled *Viking!*, based on Norse exploration and settlement of the New World. The production included over one hundred individuals, took place in a specially built concrete amphitheater, and attracted over 48,000 viewers in its two-season run. The production cost well over a million dollars and won hundreds of thousands of dollars in grants from private foundations and Minnesota. Michlovic (1990:105) notes that, "the published program lists as donors close to 500 individuals and businesses, including resorts, department stores, funeral parlors, hospitals, groceries, hardware stores, and banks."

from their predecessors. McClurg and Hewett did much that no present-day archaeologist would even consider undertaking. There is much that they believed about the past that is quite contrary to today's canon of archaeological knowledge. The past is archaeology's focus, but past research is often seen as stagnating, lagging, and holding back present and future understanding. All of the social sciences recognize the value in questioning the roots of one's discipline and searching for an explicit understanding of how explanation, reasoning, or interpretation has previously fallen short. Critique of both the hypothesis and the individual advocating it has long been part of academic archaeology. Thus, McClurg's or Hewett's backing of the Manitou cliff dwellings carries only limited weight with modern scholars. Even Hewett (1930) cautioned students to check their speculations, "regardless of where they have obtained their preparation for anthropological and archaeological research," and remember that, "their real teachers must be the Indians themselves."

The Indians Hewett spoke of were—and still are to some—considered akin to the artifacts to which archaeology grants special value. They are supposed to have a timelessness and essential qualities that different observers can go back to and verify at different times. Artifacts are supposed to be more enduring than either the ideas they generate or the people who study them. In a sense, archaeology can let its practitioners be passed by as theories change, facts are reexamined in new light, and new artifacts are uncovered. Professionals attempt to live up to the responsibilities we take on in exploring the past through self-reflexive critique. We try to explain things with a disdain for dogma. Archaeologists thus depend on change within their discipline. Professionals use it to separate themselves from previously widespread, but now known to be mistaken ideas. We use change to validate the authority with which we speak about the past.

However, the public's view of the authority of archaeology—be it any particular archaeologist's authority or the discipline's as a whole—doesn't always match our high-minded intentions. There are those who nearly beatify any archaeologist and whatever claims we make. There are those who simply take archaeologist's statements at face value, those who argue with them, those who refuse to believe, and those who aren't even listening. More is at play here than just the belief in the accuracy of either stories generated about the past or any particular fact. What archaeologists do and how we express ourselves also has a significant impact on how our ideas are received. A presentation's form affects people's willingness to view archaeologists as authorities. But the professional practices meant to serve as review are often misunderstood by the general population. Attempts to render authority via self- or peer-review only count for so much outside academia. Authoritative claims are often misconstrued as dogmatic or single-voiced statements when, in fact, they were formed through consensus and debate. Many archaeologists have come to realize that how we communicate with those outside our discipline can have tremendous impacts on it. Many archaeologists attempt to speak to the public in an intelligible way. But not everyone does this nor do all attempts at good communication always work.

Simple Answers and Camaraderie

A comparison between the Manitou cliff dwellings and other forms of archaeological fakery is useful for understanding how public reaction is based on more than just the validity of facts. Consideration of archaeological others—those amateurs, pseudo-scientists, hoaxsters, and cult archaeologists outside the traditional scholarly circle—can tell us much about what might be going on at Manitou Springs. Beliefs of the archaeological other run the gamut from simple misconceptions about artifacts (for example, mistaken ideas about how stone projectile points were crafted) to larger, incorrect assumptions about cultural processes or human nature (various Romans, Lost Tribes of Israel, Phoenicians, Chinese, and Celts in the New World prior to Columbus) to claims that defy human action and depend on the supernatural (creationism, intelligent design, or aliens building pyramids). In general, these beliefs share a common denominator: they provide simple answers to complex questions.

William Stiebing, Jr. (1987) notes that the simple explanations of archaeological others function, "in the way myth does in a primitive culture... it resolves psychological dilemmas and provides answers for the unknown or unknowable." But it is folly to consider these simple answers merely the domain of simpletons. Over many years, various groups of archaeologists have polled the public about their beliefs. Different studies have repeatedly confirmed that beliefs in archaeological others or fringe archaeology are relatively widely held—even among educated and critically aware groups like college students. These tendencies appear inherent in human nature as a psychologically satisfying function of our dealings with uncertainty.

There is something essentially comforting when questions about the past are answered in definitive ways. Moreover, one group of researchers (Taylor, Eve, and Harrold 1995) has discovered that people are apt to accept different levels of explanation in different social situations. For example, the same individual may differently accept complexity in and outside the classroom. The same individual may consider an archaeology professor an authority about the past in one instance and someone else, perhaps a creationist preacher who puts forth a contradictory idea, to be authoritative in another case. The influence of simple answers feeds off this situation. Inauthentic archaeologies often offer seemingly straightforward answers. In contrast, archaeology and professional scholarship offer the uncertainty of self-critique and even the occasional severing of ties to its own past. When archaeologists counteract dogma through self-reflexivity on one hand, we may actually be fueling skepticism on the other.

Often the tendency of archaeological others to seek and offer simple explanations is also coupled with what John Cole (1980) has identified as "ambivalent anti-elitism." This is a process in which individuals vilify the elite, ruling establishment while, at the same time, professing inordinate respect and envy for it. Stiebing (1987) has found that nonprofessional archaeologists often criticize professional scholars as being "so blindly committed to a prevailing dogmatic view that they cannot recognize the validity of new concepts," while "almost always point[ing] with pride to any support they receive from members of the Establishment." They see themselves as underdogs with special knowledge that the scholarly world refuses to accept. They see themselves as modern-day descendants of researchers like Galileo or the geologists that found evidence for continental drift who were ignored, scoffed at, and even persecuted in their own time, but eventually came to be accepted and honored by the establishment. They see themselves as those ahead of their time on whom history will look back on most kindly. Of course, nonprofessional and archaeological others are rarely persecuted or even ignored. Many academic archaeologists have complained that fringe archaeologists sell more books and appear more frequently on television than they do.

What makes ambivalent anti-elitism so attractive also helps explain why it is not just what professionals generate as facts, but how we communicate them, that is so important. Simple answers are one draw, but the community of archaeological others is another.

Unfortunately, the processes of academic credentials and scholarly communication that serve professionals so well in validating stories about the past also separates scholars from the world at large. In contrast, groups of fakers or archaeological others are both accepting of new members and seemingly special. There are still hoops to jump through and jargon to learn when talking about the past with those outside academia. But archaeological others don't require nearly as many credentials to participate. In fact, there are even examples of people who advocate contradictory forms of fringe archaeology bonding over their shared dislike of professional archaeology. Stiebing (1987) explains that:

> Desire to be part of a community that possess special knowledge may be bound up with the antiestablishment facet of cult archaeology. Organizations whose members share secret rituals, arcane knowledge, and mysterious symbols have long been popular. They supply a sense of belonging, of community identity, that many members cannot find elsewhere. In the same way, those who accept cult archaeology become part of a special community.

Prestion Peet, a popular-audience archaeology book editor who *isn't* an archaeologist, has noted the same sense of community as well (quoted in Lovata 2005).

A sense of camaraderie is a powerful thing and can even trump fact and logical reasoning. It all goes back to how people decide to accept a story of archaeology as authoritative. Professional archaeologists have a community standard of good scholarship, but theirs isn't the only community. There are those who, although quite willing to accept the ideas of professional archaeologists, don't respond well to a professional authority they see as belittling, unresponsive, or lacking in ability to reach out to or include them. There are those who side with the underdogs or nonprofessionals simply because the odds are against them. Researchers Taylor, Eve, and Harrold (1995) found people willing to hold contradictory ideas and accept as authoritative contradictory archaeologies in different social situations. The social context of an idea about the past has tremendous influence on whether that idea, or the individual advocating it, is believed.

Do the cliff dwellings at Manitou Springs tell a simple story and foster a sense of camaraderie? The signs scattered around the site, captions on the display cases, and the brochure given to each admission-paying visitor are all written in a straightforward and authoritative tone. They tell visitors what happened with firm dates and describe the uses of individual objects or rooms within the cliff dwellings in unequivocal terms. For instance, one sign indicates exactly how many families lived in a particular structure. Another sign boldly explains that there has been no real cultural change in Native Americans in the time between the fourteenth-century abandonment of the Anasazi settlements, the arrival of Spanish explorers three centuries later, and our world today. Older stories about, and older research into, the Anasazi are presented without reflexive qualifications. The museum's displays are obviously not new, but the stories they present seem almost timeless. The museum's gift shop sells a self-published $1.29 pamphlet that presents a more detailed description of the site, but it lacks a publication date that might put it into context. The Anasazi are presented as a complete story about which current research is almost unnecessary. Visitors aren't given a feeling that new finds or new perspectives will change the stories being told here. But visitors leave Manitou Springs feeling they know the Anasazi (whether or not the story presented is accurate is another matter). It is also important to note that the Manitou Springs Cliff Dwelling Museum, and ambivalent antielitism in general, validate past scholars in the present. In contrast, professional archaeology doesn't necessarily revere the influential figures, such as Virginia McClurg or "El Toro" Hewett, in its past. Professional archaeology's dependence on change and reflexive turns may actually be reinforcing those who offer claims of tradition.

The camaraderie at Manitou Springs is more subtle. The site's original builders and supporters are no longer alive and personally able to welcome anyone into a discussion of the archaeology. But there are guides available, tourists can talk to the Native American dancers, and the employees manning cash registers in the gift shop are quite willing to answer questions, the validity of their answers not withstanding. The tourists themselves are friendly with each other—taking your picture when you ask, directing you to the most interesting parts of the site, and sharing what they've learned. But a sense of camaraderie may come most from the cliff dwellings themselves. They set up situations in which the tourist is able to participate in constructing the past. They are open and accepting of visitors.

Figure 3.4 An Open Site

The Manitou cliff dwellings are accessible to all manner of visitor; even the family dog is allowed. Visitors can freely walk through nearly all the rooms, which contain signs describing the building's different uses and methods of construction. Tourists are allowed not only to look but to touch and feel the site as well.

The Role of Accessibility in Presenting the Past

The accessibility of being able to join a community of archaeologists is related to the accessibility of the archaeological record itself. Just as a community of archaeological others may be easier to join than the academic one, the fake may be more attractive than the real because it might be more inviting and more accessible.

The Manitou cliff dwellings are nothing if not accessible. They were specifically constructed along the busy Front Range to be more easily reached than sites like Mesa Verde or Chaco Canyon, which today still lie far out in a remote corner of the region. Moreover, Manitou is an interactive site (figure 3.4). The rooms within the rock shelter itself are available for not just viewing, but touching. Mesa Verde National Park contains many hundreds of different Anasazi sites, but most are closed to unguided visits and are not easy to reach. One of

Figure 3.5 Look, but Don't Touch

Mesa Verde National Park eagerly hosts visitors, but most of the park's archaeology is open for only looking. This picture of Mesa Verde from the summer of 2004 shows the contrast between a park with a mission to both present and preserve and the Manitou cliff dwellings, whose owners have no qualms about tourists physically interacting with the entire site.

Mesa Verde's most popular and accessible sites is the cliff dwelling called Spruce Tree House. Tourists can walk around this site, yet all but a single reconstructed kiva room is closed to actual entry (figure 3.5). In contrast, the copy of Spruce Tree House at Manitou Springs is open to all manner of intrusions. Steps and ramps, with sturdy hand rails, lead from the parking lot directly into the site. Once visitors to Manitou have paid their admission—which they can conveniently do before they even leave their car—they can enter nearly every room with or without a guide. They can run their fingers across the walls, sit on rock ledges, climb wooden ladders through windows and up to balconies, and actually feel the architecture. Entering into an ancient room can bring one into community with the Anasazi, but the rooms at Manitou Springs are far more accessible than those at Mesa Verde. There are no required guides, no rules against touching the site, and no one to keep people apart from the past.

Of course, restrictions against handling the past are rarely arbitrary. Mesa Verde offers a more structured and restrictive tour, in part, because the park has to preserve as well as display. It was given the mission of not only showing off a cultural wonder to all manner of visitors, but keeping the unique archaeology in place and away from destruction. A crush of visitors can quite literally grind the archaeological record into dust. In contrast, the Manitou cliff dwellings may preserve and promote the idea of the Anasazi, but they certainly aren't preserving any Anasazi artifacts in place.

The process of touching, or physically experiencing, is a particularly important part of building connections with prehistory. People crave physical contact with the past. They want a first-hand experience instead of just looking at pictures someone else took or reading someone else's observations. Diane Barthel, in her studies of cultural attractions (1996), has found that all manner of museums are attuned to the fact that deep interactivity is a necessity to avoid boring, or even driving off, the visitors. Successful cultural attractions don't simply present display case labels for visitors to read. Visitors are treated to a physical experience: from seeing guides in period dress to dressing up in period pieces themselves. Successful museums let tourists judge the heft of artifacts in their own hands, hear the clanking of antique tools at work, and actually taste the foodstuffs that nourished past generations. But this interactivity shouldn't be seen as merely an attempt to add extras to entertain or satisfy the consumer desires of the visitors. Touch can be quite simple and ultimately fundamental—not an extra embellishment. Archaeologist David Hurst Thomas (2002:132) explains that there is power in "unembellished anthropological 'things'," because they "explained clearly, anchor us culturally to the rest of the world and to our own past." Objects have a draw because they seem real and objective. Moreover, the pull of tangible things isn't just felt by tourists for whom artifacts are a unique experience. Most archaeologists, if they did not themselves feel the attraction, have encountered a colleague who felt an attraction to simply being in the field, digging in the dirt, experiencing sites first-hand, and beholding artifacts in the archaeological context.

But one shouldn't think that Thomas's "unembellished anthropological things" includes only authentic artifacts. The attraction of experience is such that the act of holding an artifact or physically walking through a site may actually trump whether or not that object or place is authentic. This is most significant when considering the fake Anasazi of Manitou Springs. Lipe (2002) notes that the tourists he leads to archaeology sites are interested in which parts have been reconstructed and which are original. Yet he also recognizes that reproductions, restorations, and virtual representations are effective at developing larger contexts and helping the public connect to the past. They are especially successful when visitors believe them to be credible reproductions or representations of the original. Barthel (1996) likewise notes that visitors to reconstructed historic sites care about the end result. They want to know that a museum or display got things right. They can have a transcendent experience with a reproduced past if they believe in the past being presented. It's not that these visitors don't value the truth or are unimpressed with original artifacts. It's that, at places like museums and archaeology sites, they want to experience the past with a full suite of senses and will accept inauthentic things if they allow for extensive interaction.

Conclusions about the Fake Anasazi

The authenticity of an object or place has a role in archaeology, but it is by no means the only force at work when telling stories about the past. People do find authentic things to be authoritative, but authority stems from more than just facts themselves. It is generated by specific actions and the senses, of community and visceral experience, they influence. Historical preservationist Diane Barthel (1996) explains that:

> determining absolute authenticity becomes a more metaphysical than practical exercise. What is more productive is to understand what different social actors—preservationists, politicians, developers, publics— think is authentic and why authenticity matters to them, if, indeed, it does matter. Historic structures may be resources for shaping collective memories, but what we make of them is up to us.

The Manitou cliff dwellings are fake. Yet, even if the information presented there is wrong or out of date, they are still an effective representation of the Anasazi. The site is a popular cultural attraction that has successfully drawn in tourists for over a century. Understanding how this site has lasted so long helps explain how archaeology itself persists. The Manitou cliff dwellings are fake, but they are tied to the history of U.S. archaeology. They were created in response to a rising interest in the Anasazi and feelings that Anasazi archaeology played an important role in how Colorado, the greater Southwest, and America at large would be defined. Manitou Springs continues to attract visitors with an authoritative story about the Anasazi. This story is told with straightforward descriptions and, more importantly, open and accessible displays. The Manitou cliff dwellings are more than archaeology on display; they are a physical experience of the past. The cliff dwellings at Manitou Springs show that the context of a presentation is a powerful force even if the story told is factually suspect. Archaeological remains do not speak for themselves, nor are inauthentic archaeologies readily dismissible simply because they are fakes. They are what we, and what we want, to make of them.

References and Further Reading

Anderson, E.G.
1999   *American Indian Literature & the Southwest*. University of Texas Press, Austin.

Barthel, D.
1996 .   *Historic Preservation: Collective Memory and Historical Identity*. Rutgers University Press, New Brunswick, New Jersey.

Berg, C.M.
2002   *Manitou Cliff Dwellings: For Education or Profit?* Paper presented at the 67th Annual Meeting of the Society for America Archaeology, Denver.

Cole, J.R.
1980   Cult Archaeology and Unscientific Method and Theory. In *Advances in Archaeological Method and Theory, volume 3*. M.B. Shiffer, editor. Academic Press, New York.

Cordell, L.S.
1984   *Prehistory of the Southwest*. Academic Press, Orlando, Florida.

1994   *Ancient Pueblo Peoples*. Smithsonian Books, Washington, D.C.

Ellis, R.
1997   The Changing Image of the Anasazi World in the American Imagination. In *Anasazi Architecture and American Design*. B.H. Morrow and V.B. Price, editors. University of New Mexico Press, Albuquerque.

Feder, K.L.
2002   *Frauds, Myths, and Mysteries: Science and Pseudoscience in Archaeology*. Fourth Edition. McGraw-Hill Mayfield, Boston.

Fowler, D.D.
2000   *A Laboratory for Anthropology: Science and Romanticism in the American Southwest*. University of New Mexico Press, Albuquerque.

Hewett, E.L.
1930   *Ancient Life in the American Southwest*. The Bobbs-Merrill Company, Indianapolis.

Holand, H.R.
1910   First Authoritative Investigation of Oldest Document in North America. *Journal of American History* 3:165–184.

1932   *The Kensington Stone: A Study in Pre-Columbian American History*. Privately printed, Ephraim, Wisconsin.

1935   The "Myth" of the Kensington Stone. *The New England Quarterly* 8(1):42–62.

1946   *America 1355-1364: A New Chapter in Pre-Columbian History*. Duell, Sloan and Pearce, New York.

1962   *A Pre-Columbian Crusade to America*. Twayne, New York.

Leonard, R.D.
1999   *Tourism—"Real" and Contrived*. http://www.unm.edu/~rleonard/230.htm.

Lipe, W.D.
2002   Public Benefits of Archaeological Research. In *Public Benefits of Archeology*. B. Little, editor. University Press of Florida, Gainesville.

Lovata, T.R.
2005   Curious Archaeology: The Process of Assembling a Fringe Prehistory. *Public Archaeology* 4(4):266–275.

Michlovic, M.
1990 Folk Archaeology in Anthropological Perspective. *Current Anthropology* 31(1):103–107.

1991 On Archaeology and Folk Archaeology: A Reply. *Current Anthropology* 32(3):321–322.

Smith, D.A.
2002   *Mesa Verde National Park: Shadows of the Centuries*. University of Colorado Press, Boulder.

Stiebing, W.H., Jr.
1987   The Nature and Danger of Cult Archaeology. In *Cult Archaeology and Creationism*. F.B. Harrold and R.A. Eve, editors. University of Iowa Press, Iowa City.

Taylor, J.H., R.A. Eve, and F.B. Harrold
1995   Why Creationists Don't Go to Psychic Fairs: Differential Sources of Pseudoscientific Beliefs. *Skeptical Inquirer* 19(6):23–28.

Thomas, D.H.
2002   Roadside Ruins: Does America Still Need Archaeology Museums? In *Public Benefits of Archeology*. B. Little, editor. University Press of Florida, Gainesville.

Weixelman, J.O.
2004   *Hidden Heritage: Pueblo Indians, National Parks, and the Myth of the "Vanishing Anasazi."* Unpublished doctoral dissertation, Department of History, University of New Mexico, Albuquerque.

Critical Questions and Exercises

1. We all depend on others to explain the past to us in meaningful and cogent ways. But have you ever questioned the validity of what you're told when visiting a museum or archaeological site? Have you ever asked who wrote the interpretive signs and labels? Have you ever asked why they chose to explain things in a particular way or even chose to display particular items at all? Have you ever asked if the artifacts on display are the originals or merely copies? Study what has driven you to ask, or kept you from asking, these types of questions. Furthermore, think about whether it matters to you that a site or artifact on display if the original or not.

2. Take this book along next time you visit an archaeology museum and compare what you see there to how the past is presented at Manitou Springs. Consider whether the museum seems successful and the displays appear attractive in the same way that they do at Manitou. Are visitors allowed to interact with artifacts in the same ways? Or do visitors have physically different experiences? Look around at other visitors and see if they are acting in ways visitors to Manitou Springs do. What do these similarities and differences tell you about how the display of archaeology affects people? What do they indicate about the role of inauthentic archaeology?

3. Although the cliff dwellings at Manitou Springs are interesting enough in and of themselves, it's also important to understand them in a wider context of other inauthentic archaeologies. Give some thought to what differentiates the Manitou Springs cliff dwellings from the Piltdown Hoax discussed in the previous chapter. Is the Manitou Springs site the same kind of deliberate fraud or should it be understood as a different kind of fake? Are there differences in how professional archaeologists were, or still are, involved in each? Are there differences in how the wider public reacted and continues to react to one in contrast to the other?

CHAPTER 4

MARKING CULTURE: TORREÓN AS CULTURAL ICON

Artifacts are themselves mute. They are meaningful only when uncovered, studied, cataloged, and displayed in the present. Handling and holding them gives them significance. Yet not all artifacts are accorded the same level of meaning. Both professional archaeologists and the general public consider specific artifacts to have reached an iconic status in our perception of prehistory. We view them as more than an example of a particular technological or ritual practice. They have come to signify entire groups of people and whole ways of life—both for prehistory and for people today. Cultural icons have a special place in understanding inauthenticity and accuracy. They refer to more than themselves and their meanings may override their origins.

Figure 4.1 Torreón outside Trujillo, Spain

This torreón is one of a pair situated along a ridge that skirts the city of Trujillo, Spain. Torreóns, or watchtowers, were defensive structures meant to serve as both look-outs and refuges of last resort. They are found across Spain and were built by many different groups over the centuries. Nevertheless, most torreóns share attributes of construction—conical shape, multiple floors, diminutive windows and doors, and massive stone walls—indicative of a common purpose.

Figure 4.2 Torreóns as Cultural Markers

This torreón, which is in line of sight with the one pictured in figure 4.1, overlooks the ruins of an extensive Roman bath. Trujillo, known in Roman times as Turgalium, is a walled city. It—like the country of Spain as a whole—has been shaped by successive waves of incoming Celtic, Roman, Visigoth, Jewish, Moorish, Christian, African, and Gallic peoples. Trujillo's architecture—the torreóns, the ramparts, the walls, its castle, and its location atop a massive granite prominence—reflects the conflict that often accompanied these cultural contacts. Archaeologists and historians have shown that groups interacted with and influenced each other even in the midst of struggles. One group did not simply overpower and replace another in Spain. Remnants of culture survived even the brutal upheavals of the Reconquista and the physical expulsion of the Jews and Muslims from the Iberian Peninsula. Even the victors were changed by the experience and Spanish material culture reflects as much.

Many artifacts and features are common both here and in other regions, but they take on particular meaning in a Spanish context. They have been transformed into cultural icons and have become a symbolic marker of people's Spanish heritage. Torreóns are one feature that has achieved such iconic status.

The sixteenth, seventeenth, and eighteenth centuries saw a great outpouring of people from Spain into the Americas. Particularly large numbers of men left the city of Trujillo and the surrounding state of Extremadura to make their fortunes in the New World. Trujillo was the home of famous and infamous conquistadors like Francisco Pizarro, Hernando Pizarro, Francisco de Orellana, and Diego Garcia de Paredes. They, along with lesser-known colonists and settlers, brought into the Americas the trappings of culture that centuries of conflict had come to define as particularly Spanish. Their ways of thinking and their self-definition became manifest in what they built in colonized lands.

Image courtesy of the Library of Congress, Prints and Photographs Division, Historic American Buildings Survey, HABS NM, 29-MANZ, 1-4.

Figure 4.3 An Outpost in Manzano, New Mexico

This photograph of a torreón in the village of Manzano in central New Mexico was taken by Jesse Nussbaum for the Museum of New Mexico in 1916. At the time, this image was taken, historian Ralph Emerson Twitchell (1917:496) explained that, "this tower is characteristic of similar structures still to be found at points that in the olden days were outposts of Spanish settlements."

Icons and Iconography

When people think of icons and archaeology they often bring up religious iconography—primarily the gilded images, embroidered textiles, and ornately rendered statues of Orthodox Christian saints. These are certainly a significant type of icon and scholars like Michael Herzfeld (1990), Margaret Kenna (1985), and Roelof von Straten (1994) have explored how religious iconography develops and functions. However, Aaron Betsky (1997:23) observes that, "what makes something into an icon varies from time to time and from place to place," and that, whereas it used to be religion or myth that defined them, "these days it is often as not advertising or corporate public relations." A corporate basis, of course, does not mean that icons are now the solely objects of commerce. After all, scholars like Steven Flutsky (1997) show that the general public tends to imbue commercial objects with meaning beyond their intended purposes similar to people's employment of religious icons in ways and for reasons different from a church's sanction (Herzfeld 1990; Kenna 1985). Nonetheless, in the contemporary world—of which both professional and public archaeologies are undeniably a part—it is commerce that most often sets icons into play.

David Nye (1997:93) notes that iconic objects, "seem to resist the flow of time, and yet they are products of a particular historical moment." They are meaningful portions of the archaeological record—tangible, recordable survivals that people often find worthy of study and preservation. They, like all artifacts, can be windows into the past and give archaeologists the opportunity to contemplate bygone lifeways. But the informative value of these objects is increased by their iconic status. Icons have meaning, either retained or newly granted, well after their initial use and they function as more than just data for studies of the past. Aaron Betsky (1997:23) explains that:

> These are, after all, artifacts: we have made them, and in that making lies a little piece of us. Icons, however, are artifacts that represent the artifactual nature of our world while they perform their specific tasks. They are not used up by use. As objects, they fit into our hands, and as spaces they contain us. Something remains even after we are finished using them. In ways that we cannot put our fingers on, they remind us of our bodies, our past, other human beings, and our future.

Icons allude to ideals of perfection, but they begin as objects of everyday life—which then become the lasting reminders through which people build memory and around which we project the possibilities of how the future might unfold.

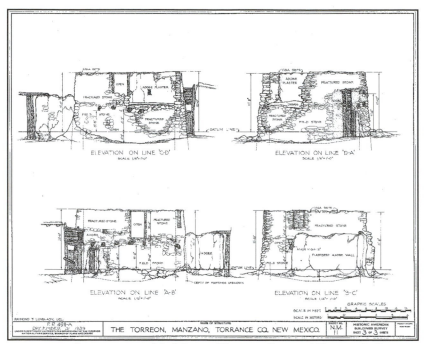

Image courtesy of the Library of Congress, Prints and Photographs Division, Historic American Buildings Survey, HABS NM, 29-MANZ, 1-.

Figure 4.4 The Torreón in Manzano

Historians have long been interested in torreóns because they represent Spanish culture in the Americas. Spanish explorers first entered New Mexico in the 1530s and permanent colonists began arriving in 1598. They brought cultural practices rooted in the Iberian Peninsula, including the construction of torreóns. Settlers continued to build them well into the 1800s, even after Mexico gained its independence from Spain and New Mexico became a territory of the United States.

Yet the torreóns, just like the settlers who erected them, changed in this new land. Most were built as defense against Native Americans, but many incorporated raw materials and construction methods indigenous to the region. This plan drawing of the Manzano torreón was made in 1939 by Raymond T. Lovelady based on the measurements made by Trent Thomas, architect in charge of the Southwest Unit of the Historic American Buildings Survey. It shows how settlers used adobe and adobe plaster alongside masonry. Adobe or mud construction was known in this region for nearly two thousand years, primarily in the form of puddled adobe walls, mud plastered over stone, and jacal (mud laid over a wooden framework). Adobe brick construction—using mud bricks shaped in wooden forms or *terrone* bricks cut from sod—was a technique brought north by Spanish colonists who had learned the practice in Mexico (McHenry 1984). Oral histories and a tree-ring sample from one of the supporting *vigas* or beams collected by the Historic American Buildings Survey indicate that the Manzano torreón was built by settlers sometime around 1840 (Thomas 1940).

Figure 4.5 A Torreón in Lincoln, New Mexico

This region was a Spanish province for over two hundred years, but few torreóns built by New Mexico's Spanish settlers are still standing today. Examples from the seventeenth and eighteenth centuries are especially rare. Many of New Mexico's torreóns persist because of active preservation or outright restoration. This watchtower in Lincoln (formerly Las Placitas), New Mexico, was built in 1855. In the 1930s, the Chaves County Archaeological and Historical Society rebuilt and marked site and eventually it became part of the Lincoln

State Monument. The United States Department of the Interior named Lincoln a National Historic Landmark in 1984, and fourteen years later the Federal Highway Commission designated Highway 380, which runs through the town and past the torreón, a National Scenic Byway. Each of these designations—from community to state to federal recognition—grants the site a certain level of credibility.

A sign stands prominently in front of the Lincoln Torreón. The text on it explains the tower's historic value and that it has been restored and is not completely original. Archaeologist William Lipe (2002:22) observes that, "paradoxically, public confidence in the accuracy of a reproduction seems to be enhanced if there also is confidence that reproductions are labeled for what they are."

Figure 4.6 The Excavated Foundation of a Torreón at the Quarai

This circular stone foundation is all that remains of a torreón that stood next to the early fifteenth-century Franciscan mission church and *convento* of La Purisima Concepción. The mission of Quarai— made up of the church, the *convento*, the torreón, and the pueblo where

Native Americans lived—is now part of the Salinas Pueblo Missions National Monument just outside Punta de Agua, New Mexico. The mission and the entire surrounding province were abandoned by the Spanish in the Pueblo Revolt of 1680. A number of archaeological investigations have been undertaken at the site since 1913 and they note that various people reoccupied the grounds over the next three centuries (Wilson 1992). The torreón at Quarai is thought to have been built by Hispanic farmers sometime in the mid-1800s. This foundation and the rest of the mission, like the Lincoln Torreón, have undergone repeated and major repair, restoration, and stabilization over the last seventy-five years.

Figure 4.7 The Visitor's Center at Quarai

Quarai was designated a state monument before it became part of the Salinas Pueblo Missions National Monument. In 1971, prior to the assumption of federal control, state funds were allocated to build a visitor's center at the site. The architects of Ted C. Luna & Associates designed the center as clear reference to a colonial-era torreón. The visitor's center is an example of programmatic architecture, in which a building bluntly represents what's offered to those who come inside. The use of a torreón both reflects and reinforces the structure's role as a cultural icon.

The stories presented to the national monument's visitors—in brochures, in guide books, on labels and signs, in models reconstructing the site, and in conversation with docents and rangers—are backed by the credibility of government sanction similar to that at Lincoln. But the Quarai visitor's center also represents a shift away from the level of authenticity conferred on a rebuilt or reconstructed feature. This building is not a replica of form. Instead, it is the reworking of a concept, held in the present, about people and material culture from the past. As scholar Erin Addison (2004) demonstrates, icons are not entirely accurate statements or detailed testaments. Instead, they are part of a cultural shorthand that amplifies and simplifies what we today consider important and meaningful about what came before us.

Figure 4.8 Public Art at Torreón Park, Santa Fe, New Mexico

The lack of readily visible torreóns has actually heightened their iconic status. The aptly named Torreón Park in Santa Fe, New Mexico, contains a stone, concrete, and tile monument in the shape of a Spanish watchtower. The park takes it name from the surrounding neighborhood, the barrio El Torreón, which itself was named after a now missing torreón built in the area during Spanish colonial times.

Figure 4.9 Public Art Is What a People Believe and Value, Made Material

In 1993, Santa Fe, New Mexico's 1% for the Arts Program erected artist Pedro Romero's sculpture "El Torreón del Barrio del Torreón" in Torreón Park. This commemorated both the torreón and the pastoral lifestyle that defined the barrio up until the twentieth century. The painted tiles encircling the top of the piece portray a range of people and activities. It should surprise no one that the original torreón and the idea of defense are prominently displayed. One set of tiles form an early eighteenth-century vignette of armed Spanish women on the lookout for Indians and standing ready to take refuge in the tower.

Lipe (2002) has explained that re-creations and replicas are effective when people believe them credible. No one would mistake this monument for the original torreón that once stood nearby. This is not a replica or re-creation. It is a referent rather than an original artifact. But public art is more than just the outdoor display of an individual artist's work. It is an affirmation of specific values and specific beliefs. Public art is granted special standing as an explicit expression of the community and the government that erected it. The fact that this monument is prominently situated in a public park gives it credibility. The piece is also clearly marked with a plaque that explains the role of the original torreón, the role of Spanish settlers in colonial New Mexico, and the role of the city in commemorating both. When Santa Fe commissioned this piece, it validated particular stories about the past and celebrated specific heritages.

Figure 4.10 The Symbolic Architecture of the National Hispanic Cultural Center

The Barelas neighborhood in Albuquerque, New Mexico's South Valley is home to the twenty-two-acre campus of the National Hispanic Cultural Center. The center was designed to reference traditional Hispanic building techniques, encompass the diversity that is a Hispanic heritage, and embody the idea of Hispanic people's enduring presence in the Americas (Lopez et al. 1999).

Each structure on this site has meaning. Stacked block wall façades are reminiscent of Quarai and other missions in the Salinas valley. The sloping steps that run the height of the main building evoke Mexican pyramids. Arched hallways and interior courtyards mimic innumerable buildings across Spain: from Zaragossa's Aljafería in the north to Granada's Alhambra in the south. A snaking fountain, whose path is paralleled by the flags of all Spanish-speaking countries, recalls the *acequias*, or irrigation ditches central to agriculture and settlement. An adobe school house that has been remodeled into a library and genealogy center reminds visitors that the campus was once the heart of the Hispanic community of Barelas. Of course, there is a torreón as well. It is meant to "provide a point of reference, both on the site and from a distance" (Lopez et al. 1999:18). Inside the torreón, artist Federico Vigil is currently painting a giant, concave fresco—the largest in North America—that tracks the many contributions that different peoples have made to Hispanic culture.

The National Hispanic Cultural Center represents a break from other sites discussed so far. The center's architectures are not just icons of Spanish culture; they are markers of a yet wider mix of peoples, histories, and prehistories. New Mexico is no longer defined as just an outpost of the Spanish empire. Instead, it is identified as an integral part of Hispanic culture. Diverse roots have crystallized here into a label related to, but different from, Spanish. The center's torreón represents a modern and vibrant culture and not just Spanish colonial settlement. This torreón no longer protects Spaniards; instead it marks the heart of Hispanic peoples.

Figure 4.11 The Manny Aragón Torreón

The National Hispanic Cultural Center's torreón is named after its patron, state senator Manny Aragón. The senator was a long-serving and powerful force in both Albuquerque's heavily Hispanic South Valley and the state's Roundhouse. The center itself is run under the auspices of the state's Office of Cultural Affairs, which also oversees state monuments—such as that at Lincoln.

The center's torreón, like Pedro Romero's tower in Santa Fe, is only a referent and not a reconstruction. But the Manny Aragón Torreón also represents another shift away from an original archaeological feature. The Barelas neighborhood has a long history dating back to early Spanish settlement in the region; but it is not named for a torreón. No watchtower is known to have stood nearby. The center's torreón could be thought of as a physically unattached icon. It is grounded in ideas rather than the authenticity of place.

Figure 4.12 Enticing Tourists with Heritage

This billboard, on Interstate Highway 25 between Albuquerque and Santa Fe, New Mexico, invites tourists to spend the night at a local hotel. Many in Santa Fe, including the city government, explicitly use history to attract visitors. This advertisement's use of a torreón is meant to heighten the hotel's appeal by aligning it with a sense of culture depth. However, The Lodge at Santa Fe is not recognized as a historic building. Its torreón is entirely new. It has neither a direct connection to any specific watchtower nor any oversight—by either an archaeologist or a government's cultural entity—in either its design or presentation.

Archaeologists tend to find advertising that makes use of archaeology to be problematic. Most are like Terry Goddard (2002:13), who supports the public display of archaeological symbols because they believe that, "this kind of exposure is the critical wedge for entering the public consciousness." Yet Lauren Talalay (2004:215) also speaks for many archaeologists—Goddard included—when she observes that most advertisements that use archaeological icons, "are not entirely satisfactory," "tend to trivialize the past," and "could benefit from a heavy dose of 'editing'." Talalay goes on to ask her colleagues to consider what kind of archaeo-advertising they would create instead. Anthropologist Traci Ardren (2004) advocates an even more extreme position because she claims that advertising tends to separate people from their rightful cultural patrimony. She calls on professional archaeologists to demand that advertisers refrain from using archaeological images that lack educational value or which fail to demonstrably support local and indigenous communities.

This presents a problem—the issue is one of control. Archaeologists are used to using their unique knowledge and skill in judging prehistory. We have much training that allows us to be sought out as experts. Archaeologists also have plenty of first-hand experience with what happens when archaeological symbols are deemed insensitive or even offensive. But icons of the past have a tendency to slip through any professional constraints. Very few marketers appear to regularly consult heritage professionals.

Figure 4.13 The McDonald's Restaurant in the Barelas Neighborhood

This McDonald's restaurant, with its watchtower-shaped entrance, is located directly across the street from the National Hispanic Cultural Center in Albuquerque, New Mexico. It appears to be another example of archaeology advertising something that is not actually an artifact or an archaeology site. Like The Lodge at Santa Fe, it appears to be an inauthentic structure made without professional oversight.

Figure 4.14 Continuity at McDonald's

Appearances alone can be deceiving. In fact, the McDonald's torreón and the one across the street at the National Hispanic Cultural Center have much in common. There is a shared vision behind each construction. Both were built as part of a conscious revitalization of the economically depressed, historically Hispanic neighborhood of Barelas. Both torreóns were built as iconic references to culture rather than as archaeologically accurate reconstructions of a local site.

Both were constructed through the careful study of New Mexico's, the Barelas neighborhood's, and Hispanic people's histories. The restaurant franchisee actually consulted with the National Hispanic Cultural Center in adorning the restaurant. Numerous historic photographs of the Barelas neighborhood and its vibrant Hispanic community were reproduced from the center's collections for display in McDonald's.

Moreover, architect Fred Robinson, who designed the Barelas McDonald's, is employed by the architectural firm of Kells+Craig.

Majolica and Indígena Pottery in the New World

Torreóns are one seemingly timeless marker of Spanish culture that have actually shifted and changed in new environments and as time passes. Other kinds of material culture, such as Majolica and Indígena types of pottery, also reflect the complicated amalgamations that are Spanish and Hispanic in the New World. Archaeologists have traditionally focused on ceramics both because they're a sturdy material that survives well over the centuries and because their stylistic and chemical properties can often be matched to specific geographic regions and specific groups of people within well-defined time periods. Majolica ceramics are a tin-enameled, soft-paste earthenware with an opaque surface. Archaeologist Ross Jamieson (2001) and chemical engineer R.G.V. Hancock (Jamieson and Hancock 2004) explain that Majolica was originally manufactured in Renaissance-era Spain based on glaze technologies from the Near East and Italy. Spanish colonists brought this popular pottery with them into the New World, and archaeologists and art historians have long noted its early presence in Spanish households across Latin America. Gair Tourtellot (1970:138) explains that Majolica:

> is of considerable interest because it underwent rapid stylistic changes from various sources, and because of its wide distribution wherever Hispanic upper class or religious establishments were located. Indeed, its history in Spain parallels the fortunes of the Spanish empire. In the New World, to, Majolica may be an equally sensitive indicator of economic conditions.

Jamieson and Hancock (2004; Jamieson 2001) are but two of many researchers who have explored the complicated trade routes that moved Majolica between Spain and the New World and within the New World itself. They have examined how and why the pottery was also produced in places like Central Mexico, Panama, and the Andes. They note that scholars had the propensity to emphasize the Spanish ethnicity of Majolica potters and pottery users and, likewise, tended to label the producers and users of local, unglazed wares as indigenous. Contemporary researchers challenge this simple dichotomy and note the complexity of ethnic and status boundaries in colonial Latin America. Majolica, like the concept of Hispanic itself, was used in different ways as marker of power and wasn't always the exact same item in one place compared to another. Similarly, Enrique Rodriguez-Alegría, Hector Neff, and Michael Glascock (2003) have reviewed the use of Majolica's traditional antonym, earthen pots known as Indígena ware, and demonstrate that they weren't simply Indians' poor imitations of haughty Spanish ceramics.

They specialize in historic preservation, documentation, restoration, and renovation. Kells+Craig has prepared data for buildings nominated to the National Register of Historic Places, is able to produce designs that meet the stringent standards of the Historic American Buildings Survey, and has a principal who meets the U.S. Department of the Interior's qualifications for a historic architect. What may appear to be a very simple, almost stereotypical branding of a building was actually created by an architect at a firm with much expertise in considering how their designs reflect and serve community heritage.

Consultation with heritage professionals is what Lauren Talalay (2004) and Traci Ardren (2004) advocate in their studies of commercial uses of the past. But that doesn't assure a design noticeably different from one crafted by marketers alone. Only with closer study of the building's history would anyone find the most important differences between the Barelas McDonald's and other commercial uses of torreóns. But the same close examination would also show the links between it and noncommercial uses of the past as well.

Closer examinations of an artifact's development and history are especially useful undertakings. They show that an artifact is different from any number of other examples of the same. For instance, each torreón presented here is related to, but different from the other. This allows archaeologists to compare and make meaningful statements about material culture. We can see that torreón building traveled from Spain to the New World but that the idea of a torreón diffused even further. Torreóns have achieved iconic status in marking Hispanic culture. Their role as a reference to a Hispanic identity is a powerful thing—more powerful than how accurately they resemble some Ur-artifact or even each other. Torreóns have become a tool with which different individuals—artists, architects, designers, archaeologists, tourists, heritage professionals, and more—can use to mark Hispanic culture and its roots. Iconic status means that some basic attributes of form are shared, but that the details of construction can diverge quite widely. Meaning is generated in basic traits shaped for specific circumstances, not in strict adherence to details irrespective of context.

References and Further Reading

Addison, E.
2004   The Roads to Ruins: Accessing Islamic Heritage in Jordan. In *Marketing Heritage: Archaeology and the Consumption of the Past*. Y. Rowan and U. Baram, editors. AltaMira, Walnut Creek, California.

Ardren, T.
2004   Where Are the Maya in Ancient Maya Archaeological Tourism?: Advertising and the Appropriation of Culture. In *Marketing Heritage: Archaeology and the Consumption of the Past*. Y. Rowan and U. Baram, editors. AltaMira, Walnut Creek, California.

Bender, B.
1998   *Stonehenge: Making Space*. Berg, Oxford, England.

Betsky, A.
1997 The Enigma of the Thigh Cho: Icons as Magnets of Meaning. In *Icons: Magnets of Meaning*. A. Betsky, editor. Chronicle Books, San Francisco.

Flutsky, S.
1997   Icons in the Stream: On Local Revisions of Global Stuff. In *Icons: Magnets of Meaning*. Aaron Betsky, editor. Chronicle Books, San Francisco.

Goddard, T.
2002   Potsherds and Politics. In *Public Benefits of Archeology*, B. Little, editor. University of Florida Press, Gainesville.

Herzfeld, M.
1990   Icons and Identity: Religious Orthodoxy and Social Practice in Rural Crete. *Anthropological Quarterly* 63(3):109–121.

Holtorf, C.
2005   *From Stonehenge to Las Vegas: Archaeology as Popular Culture*. AltaMira, Walnut Creek, California.

Jamieson, R.W.
2001   Majolica in the Early Colonial Andes: The Role of Panamanian Wares. *Latin American Antiquity* 12(1):45–58.

Jamieson, R.W. and R.G.V. Hancock
2004   Neutron Activation Analysis of Ceramics from Southern Highland Ecuador. *Archaeometry*. 46(4): 569–583.

Kenna, M.E.
1985   Icons in Theory and Practice: An Orthodox Christian Example. *History of Religions* 24(4):345–368.

Lipe, W.D.
2002   Public Benefits of Archaeological Research. In *Public Benefits of Archeology*. B. Little, editor. University of Florida Press, Gainesville.

Lopez, D., R. Love, M. Miller, G. Saavedra, C. Vasquez, and P.M. Vattier
1999   *Building the Village: Flow of the River, Volume II*. The National Hispanic Cultural Center, Albuquerque, New Mexico

McHenry, P.G.
1984   *Adobe and Rammed Earth Buildings: Design and Construction*. The University of Arizona Press, Tucson.

Nye, D.
1997 The Cultural and Historical Roots of American Icons. In *Icons: Magnets of Meaning*. Aaron Betsky, editor. Chronicle Books, San Francisco.

Ramos Rubio, J.A.
1998   *Trujillo*. Editorial Everest, S.A., Leon, Spain.

Rodriguez-Alegría, E., H. Neff, and M. D. Glascock
2003   Indigenous Ware or Spanish Import? The Case of Indígena Ware and Approaches to Power in Colonial Mexico. *Latin American Antiquity* 14(1):67–81.

Talalay, L.E.
2004   The Past as Commodity: Archaeological Images in Modern Advertising. *Public Archaeology* 3(4):205–216.

Thomas, T.
1940   *The* Torreón *(Stone Fort): Manzano, Torrance County, New Mexico*. Historic American Buildings Survey, No. N.M.-11, Santa Fe, New Mexico.

Tourtellot, G.
1970   Spanish Majolica in the New World: Types of the Sixteenth to Eighteenth Centuries (Book Review). *Man*. New series, 5(1):138.

Twitchell, R.E.
1917   *The Leading Facts of New Mexican History, Volume IV*. The Torch Press, Cedar Rapids, Iowa.

von Straten, R.
1994   *An Introduction to Iconography.* Translated by P. de Man. Gordon and Breach, Amsterdam, The Netherlands.

Warburton, M. and P. Duke
1995   Projectile Points as Cultural Symbols. In *Beyond Subsistence: Plains Archaeology and the Post-Processual Critique.* P. Duke and M.C. Wilson, editors. University of Alabama Press, Tuscaloosa.

Wilson, J.P.
1992   *Salinas Pueblo Missions: Quarai.* Southwest Parks and Monuments Association, Tucson, Arizona.

Critical Questions and Exercises

1. What role do rarity and scarcity play in the status that people accord different artifacts? Many of the torreóns that once existed in New Mexico fell into disrepair and eventually disappeared (although the remnants of many no doubt remain underground). Are scarce artifacts more likely to be replicated, copied, and even become iconic than widely available and easily visible ones? Do people craft replicas because the originals are no longer around or because they are so widespread? To answer these questions, it may be fruitful to compare torreóns to other archaeological-based markers of culture. For instance, Miranda Warburton and Phil Duke (1995) note people associate arrowheads with Native American peoples of the Great Plains region. Arrowheads, unlike torreóns, are relatively plentiful in contemporary America. Numerous signs incorporate arrowheads and a number of arrows and arrowheads enlarged in scale into architecture itself. They join the vast array of original-size arrowheads that can be found on display and integrated into the cultural landscape.

2. Different people, groups, businesses, and governments have recognized torreóns as especially important symbols of culture and history. This type of recognition has a lot of influence on which and how artifacts become iconic. What specific status is gained from each kind of recognition? Are there differences between formal and informal acknowledgment? Consider the distinctions between groups recognizing something of themselves (such as people who commemorate their ancestors or residents acknowledging the history of their neighborhood) and outsiders according them special status (such as nonresident archaeologists identifying certain things as unique or the federal government labeling something as valuable).

3. Do you approve of the ways in which the archaeological record is used in advertising? Think about what leads you to that conclusion. First, undertake a survey of advertising and look for the archaeology. This is a relatively easy process because scholars like Traci Ardren (2004), Barbara Bender (1998), Cornelius Holtorf (2005), and Lauren Talalay (2004) have all both generated extensive inventories of archaeo-advertising and demonstrated that the form is widespread across a variety of media. Second, closely scrutinize your reactions to different advertisements and consider why you engage them as such. You might react positively, negatively, be apathetic, or fall somewhere in between. Do you respond to particular forms—broadcast versus print media—or styles—brash and colorful versus reverent and low key—of achaeo-advertising? Are your judgments based on the kind of products advertised? Could your reactions be based on your or the advertisers' status as archaeologists, students, scholars, nonscholars, direct descendants of groups who created specific segments of the archaeological record, or outsiders with only general connections to the archaeology being used?

CHAPTER 5

THREE ARTISTS ON ARCHAEOLOGY

Archaeologists have a complex relationship with art. The act of reconstructing the past is very much a visual process in which people move from looking at artifacts to envisioning wide ranges of human activity. Art has tremendous power in shaping our perceptions of prehistory. Researchers like Stephanie Moser (1998) and Troy Lovata (2005) are but two of many to have shown that art affects both how people view the past and their ideas about how archaeology is done. Scholars like Simon James, who are both archaeologists and artists report that the act of visually presenting the past is a creative and complicated course in which speculation and inference are used to fill in the many gaps in the archaeological record (1997). But archaeologists-cum-illustrators aren't the only ones who use prehistoric peoples and ancient artifacts in their art. Art doesn't just serve archaeology and archaeologists don't always control art. The works inspired by or that make use of the discipline of archaeology are not academic archaeology. They follow different conventions, live up to different responsibilities and are crafted in ways apart from academic archaeology. Understanding how and why artists create work that engages archaeology lets us see how the field is perceived. It can also show why old things have such a presence in the modern world. However, it is worthwhile not just to critique art and speculate about an artist's intentions. Letting artists explain, in their own words, why they create the art they do provides unique insight into archaeology in the service of art.

Interview Number One:
Megaliths and Monumental Ideas

Adam Horowitz is the forty-seven-year-old artist and filmmaker behind a massive, multi-year art project that draws inspiration from both the finds and the practices of archaeologists. Stonefridge/Fridgehenge is his full-scale re-creation of the famous British megalithic site of Stonehenge. The piece is being built—with the hard-won approval of the city—from hundreds of discarded refrigerators atop the Santa Fe, New Mexico, municipal dump. The work appears to be a playful artistic prank. Yet, a serious exploration of the cultural disruption wrought by technological change and a somber meditation on the arrogance of power runs through all of Adam Horowitz's art. Stonefridge/Fridgehenge is an artist's take on modern consumerism that appropriates the massive scale and undisputed renown of Stonehenge. But it's apparent that this piece is more than just a representation of an archaeology site. Its construction required an understanding of the draw of artifacts or sites and the attraction of a mysterious prehistory. Eight years into the project and halfway toward completing Stonefridge/Fridgehenge, Horowitz sat for an interview about what's driven his art and the role that archaeology plays in his life's work.

TROY LOVATA: *I know that you formally studied archaeology for a while before you turned to doing art. What's your background with archaeology and where did you study it?*

ADAM HOROWITZ: I wanted to be Indiana Jones before there was an Indiana Jones. But my idea of archaeology was going to exotic places in the Third World and digging up the tombs of kings and digging up treasure and finding artifacts that were magical. When I say treasure I don't mean because of its monetary value, I mean treasure because of its cultural value and its historical and intellectual value. All the stuff that's become comic book fodder, that was my idea of treasure, too.

T.L.: *It sounds like this precedes school; that an interest in archaeology was something you went into college with.*

A.H.: I went into college at Berkeley [the University of California] and the first course I took in anthropology was physical anthropology. For

Figure 5.1 Stonefridge/Fridgehenge

Adam Horowitz's sprawling take on Stonehenge lies atop Santa Fe, New Mexico's municipal landfill. In the background—to the west—are the Jemez Mountains and the city of Los Alamos. England's original is known for its astronomical alignments. For this piece, the artist sought out the alignment of the dump with the once-secret city where the first atomic bomb was developed as part of a statement about over-consumption and environmental destruction.

some reason, I had the passion for archaeology and physical anthropology from before that, from early on. I grew up in Hollywood, and my favorite movie growing up was the original *King Kong* (Copper and Shoedsack 1933). As a child I saw *King Kong* about a hundred times. I wanted to be Carl Denham. I wanted to go to Skull Island. I was convinced, at nine years old, that Skull Island was real. I had to find it, and if it wasn't Skull Island, it was going to be another Skull Island, and I was going to go there and find my own King Kong.

T.L.: *So you went into college with this notion from the movies, but did you have any other experiences before then?*

A.H.: I was a traveler. I went to Stonehenge when I was twelve. My mother took me to England when I was twelve. Then, as I am sure now, the number one tourist attraction was Stonehenge. You could just walk right up to it at that time. I got to Stonehenge and my jaw

Figure 5.2 Rising and Falling Megaliths

The megaliths seen today in Europe are not complete—degradation, erosion, looters, and collectors have all changed these sites. Similarly, Stonefridge/Fridgehenge is a multi-year project that appears to be both rising and falling apart at the same time. Questions of completeness or incompleteness highlight archaeological issues of preservation, reconstruction, and formation processes.

dropped. I got there, and even at twelve years old I knew something special had gone on there. I knew, even at that age, I grasped the size of these stones. I grasped the mystery and magic of that place. I was still physically small at that time and this construction towering over me, I was awestruck.

T.L.: *It seems that the past really was a whole body experience for you.*

A.H.: Yes, I knew I was in the land of the giants. I was in the land of the UFOs. I just was in heaven. I was in Stonehenge and I said, "How did they do this, why did they do this, who did this?" All those questions that we ask later as adults came to me then. It never left me, the magic of that experience. And that tied into my early childhood, things like King Kong and Jason and the Argonauts. I grew up in Hollywood and my grandfather was in the movie business. As a child I used to go to movie sets. I lived in this area near movie studios. At

Figure 5.3 Erecting a Trilithon
The artist considered it important that primitive technology be used in the construction—in this case, block and tackle instead of crane or forklift. He often further highlighted the links and contrasts between past and present by having the workers dress as slaves during construction. Reproduced courtesy of Adam Jonah Horowitz

the same time I went to Stonehenge there was an old back lot from MGM and RKO studios in Culver City that had been sold off and was going to be made into condos. My friends and I used to take our bicycles to the old back lot as they were bulldozing it. We would climb in, sneak in at the end of the workday, and we would salvage stuff. So, to me that was an archaeological site of sorts. It was the archaeology of the movies, but even at twelve years old, it was an archaeological site.

T.L.: *So even then, you placed a value on physical things from the past?*

A.H.: Absolutely, I cried when I saw them bulldozing these sets. I cursed them. I said, "What are you people nuts? This is history. This is to be preserved." I had seen the movies [made there], and that was a great adventure to me. So I think, from an early age, I always mixed Hollywood imagery and real life. I loved this fantasy world and I think that archaeology always fit into this romantic primal story of archaeology and exploration and theater. Even as a child I used to look at books and photographs of these Egyptian kings and was just amazed of the beauty and complexity of the artifacts of this amazing civilization. At the same time, I would watch *The Ten Commandments* (DeMille 1956) with Charleton Heston as Moses and Yul Brenner as the pharaoh. I would just combine it all and I would say here's the Howard Carter and the real excavation, and I would imagine the pharaoh, and of course, it's Yul Brenner. So all my life I've been combining Hollywood with history, Hollywood with archaeology. Because, it's the way we understand the past, it's through Hollywood, especially in this country. Hollywood is the re-creation of history and prehistory. But later I did actually study archaeology in college.

T.L.: *Did you ever work on any archaeology sites?*

A.H.: I did, in the Bay Area. I worked on an archaeological site of an Old West town, east of Oakland and Berkeley, California. I was a grunt; essentially on this dig because I was a college freshman and didn't know anything. I was being trained. I also worked on artifacts from Mayan sites in Guatemala. My first archaeology professor was a Guatemalan, Mayan specialist. He and his graduate student had amassed a lot of artifacts. So I had a job scrubbing artifacts. Cleaning, cataloging, labeling. I did that in the basement of Kroeber Hall at Berkeley for several months. It was a horrendous experience. I wanted to be in the jungle excavating a temple, instead I was in the basement cleaning potsherds, and the potsherds all looked identical. They weren't even painted, they weren't even polychrome, they weren't even particularly shaped. They were just boxes of potsherds and they were all just red clay. I complained to the professor and to some of his graduate students. I said, "This is ridiculous; they all look the same, they are all just this red clay." They chastised me for being bored, for being unexcited about it. They said, "This is archaeology, you better get used to it." After weeks of scrubbing, I said that if this is archaeology, forget about it. And the other thing was, I knew that it wasn't true. Even my professor . . . he had kind of an Indiana Jones kind of blood. He was kind of an eccentric fellow. One of the best stories about him was that they uncovered the tomb of a Mayan king in Guatemala, in the early seventies. Within three weeks of uncovering this tomb, there was this major earthquake that destroyed whole cities. They were brought out of Guatemala because they were blamed for causing the earthquake, for disturbing the spirits and opening this tomb. Plus, I heard stories of alcohol-fueled debauchery. Even in the basement of the archaeology department, I knew these guys had a lot more fun than I was having.

T.L.: *So did you move to the world of art because it was more fun?*

A.H.: Yes, but, you know, the other thing was the scientific method. I think I am just a liberal arts kind of guy. All rules of the scientific method, but I am not good at following rules. The whole thing with science is that there is a very rigid methodology you have to follow. And coming from a background and a passion of theater—a re-created and scripted versions of reality—this whole idea that I had to follow the scientific method, I realized after about a year, that I was not going to make a good scientist. I realized that I better get out of science and get into the liberal arts. Science was too restraining for me. If I had stayed in archaeology, I probably would have come up with the Piltdown man or something. With this bottled frustration, I would've just come up with the Piltdown man just for the fun of it.

T.L.: *Okay, so it's probably good you moved from archaeology to art. Speaking of your art, can you give us just a short description of Stonefridge/ Fridgehenge; just what it is?*

A.H.: It's an anti-monument; it's a post-apocalyptic monument to technology and consumer society. It's kind of a satiric look at the waste of this society. I say anti-monument because it is made out of trash and built on top of a dump. It is monumental size, and it is inspired by Stonehenge, which is one of the most famous archaeological sites and prehistoric monuments in the world. So, it is a monument, I just say anti-monument because it's not a celebration, it is more of a warning and a mocking of the hubris of man. To me, Stonehenge is meaningful because it predates the pyramids, and is to me a symbol and maybe even an actual manifestation of the birth of civilization. Stonehenge to me represents the birth of civilization. There was enough political and religious organization to gather the manpower and design expertise and all it took to build it. It has all the hallmarks of what we call civilization.

T.L.: *When you were putting this project together was there something other than Stonehenge you considered? Did you say, "What other large-scale things form the past could I re-create or emulate," or was it that Stonehenge just stood out?*

A.H.: You know, it was the first thing that came to mind. It wasn't like I set out to make a monument to consumer society. I was at the dump, throwing my trash away. That landfill is not open anymore, but when this all started it was a working landfill. It was a pit, a hundred feet deep. You could drive into the pit to dump your garbage. I used to go there and it was a religious experience to actually go there to see a city landfill in operation. To be able to drive into a pit, a hundred feet deep of garbage, was a religious experience. I would sort of marvel at what we throw away. I would also collect things and take them home. Invariably, I would go into the landfill to collect the garbage. I was into recovering useful things. I went there, and there was a hundred feet of garbage in the landfill, which was awesome. There were also fields of appliances. I remember, one day I went out there, and there were a hundred refrigerators out there. I couldn't believe it. Some of them looked to be in new condition. There was every vintage and every color. A lot of them, you could tell, the only reason they were there was because somebody didn't like the color, or they remodeled their kitchen, they wanted something newer. A lot of these appliances were in working order. To see all of this steel and machinery in working order, but being buried because somebody didn't like the color, or they wanted something newer, it was insane. I would say most of them appeared to be in working order. That's when I realized that something had to be done. I had to make a monument, I had to make a statement, I had to somehow, as the guy in the film *Network* (Lumet 1976) said, "Go to your window and open your window, and yell 'I am mad as hell, and I am not going to take it anymore!'" That was my moment, and I looked at it and I said, "Something had to be done with all these refrigerators." I was driving back out, and I had just left the pit and I said, "a monument, Stonehenge, I'll make Stonehenge." By the time I got to the gate of the landfill I said to myself, "They'll never allow it." I already knew it would never fly, even before I left the landfill. The idea came, and I shot it down myself, before I left. But I persevered, and I went through the city bureaucracy, and it took me about a year and a half, well over a year, to convince the bureaucrats, that this was a good idea. I had to go through every single department of the city—departments you never even knew existed.

T.L.: *I understand that when you were putting this together, physically erecting it, that you went low tech. Were you re-creating how they erected the original Stonehenge?*

A.H.: I think that whether the monument is a celebration of nature, or the planets, or the birth of civilization or the death of civilization, that there is a primal human instinct to build monuments. It's what Jung called the collective unconscious, I think. Man likes to build monuments. Whether it is Stonehenge, or the pyramids of Egypt, or the Sphinx, or Machu Picchu, or the Mayan temples, or the cathedrals of Europe, man has a need to build monuments. I think I have that same primal thrill from building a monument. I think that building it with primal technology makes it more visceral, more real. Part of the mystery of Stonehenge and the pyramids, and other prehistoric sites, is wondering how they did it. This is part of the fascination. I wanted to know what it takes to build a monument. Now we have the hydraulic cranes, the technology is there to build anything, to build skyscrapers. But I wanted to feel the weight against my back and I wanted to know the experience of organizing people to do this, and what does it take to organize humans to do this with manpower. Part of this was the physical experience of lifting all these blocks and putting them together. Part was also the experience of what it takes to organize people to do something like this.

T.L.: *Do you think that the mystery people attribute to Stonehenge comes from asking: "What does it take to move this massive stone block?"*

A.H.: Yes, that is what I felt. How do they do this? Even to this day there are theories and re-creations of Stonehenge and of how did they did it. I've seen a lot of those of those re-creations, and, frankly, they are not that convincing. To me, there are a lot of questions about Stonehenge that have not been answered. Even the age of it doesn't really seem fully understood. You know Stonehenge, still attracts thousands of people today. I think even in ancient times, long after it was completed, it still attracted people. It's a powerful place.

T.L.: *Do you mean that it's too monumental to not attract people?*

A.H.: I'm sure that over the centuries different people that come and go wanted to be buried there to be associated with this monument, even if they didn't build it. I wouldn't be surprised if all of the builders of Stonehenge were tourists. And there are the Druids. People love to associate the Druids with it, and the Druids probably came into the picture two thousand years after Stonehenge was built. Yet, to this day, the Druids come and hold rituals there. Even now, you hear people say "Oh, well, it was built with the help of aliens." You hear that kind of thing about the pyramids and other ancient sites . . . people love to talk about UFOs and strange extraterrestrial forces. That's just the example of the kind of awe these places inspire.

T.L.: *How did you go about finding what was going to be the accurate thing for you to re-create? How did you judge the authority of these different reconstructions?*

A.H.: I got every book and article I could find about Stonehenge. Plus, I had been there myself. I researched what I could, and in the end I made a judgment call based on aesthetics, my personal aesthetic. I was not really convinced by any of the scientific conclusions, so I just really went with my gut as to what I thought felt right, based on all the accounts that I had read. The actual building of it I have very often done as performance art. I dress up in costume and have my workers dress up in costume, and when I say costume, I really mean identity ... it's more than a costume. Mostly it's me as pharaoh, and the crew as the slaves. That's a recurring motif. And I have this megalomaniac priest.

T.L.: *So who, or what, are the slaves?*

A.H.: The slaves are the prehistoric reference to Stonehenge or to the pyramids. I think traditionally were probably built by slaves and so it's the prehistoric reference to that. We are creating, or re-creating, a prehistoric monument. Part of this is manpower, and who would do this but slaves? Maybe people did build them out of belief and dedication. Maybe that is possible, but in my twisted Hollywood mind, slaves are also entertaining. There is an entertainment aspect to all this too. I think it actually has driven a lot of the project. Entertainment works as a means of communication. People like to be entertained, people like to laugh. And I like to laugh as well. So, to me, a really cool way to communicate is to entertain somebody; so they leave and say, "Oh, maybe this isn't such a joke, maybe this isn't just silliness, maybe there is actually some meaning behind it." That is actually what took me out of science and into entertainment. You know there are really different ways to address the same question, and the same issues. Archaeology deals with trying to figure out what civilizations were and what made them tick and what made them thrive and what made them fail, through science and through examination of their monuments and their trash. I am looking at the same basic element: monuments and trash. I am asking what does that tell us about our society. But I am doing it from a more literary and a more entertainment angle than from a scientific angle. In a way I am examining our society the way an archaeologist does. Which is to say, "What do we worship, and what monuments should we erect, or do we erect? And what do we throw away?" So, I think I am looking at the same things as archaeologists. They love ceremonial sites and religious sites because that's supposed to be an insight into people's civilization.

T.L.: *Do you mean insight into past people's thinking?*

A.H.: Yes, what was important to them, what were their dreams and inspirations? The other thing is; I look at Stonefridge/Fridgehenge as a post-apocalyptic monument. If there was a nuclear disaster or a biological disaster, what will we leave behind? What will archaeologists in the future find of this civilization? This is kind of a joke on what they will find. Obviously, it's not going to last that long. But, in a way, when we think about the post-apocalypse, if there was a monument we would leave behind for future archaeologists, this seems like an appropriate one. What would they say about us based on it? They would say that we threw a lot of stuff away that was pretty valuable, we wasted a lot and we worshipped technology. So, in a way I am creating a phony archaeological site that, in a farcical way, is aimed at archaeologists of the future, but is also aimed at laymen of today.

Interview Number Two:
Visualizing the Bronze Age

Eric Shanower has been a professional illustrator and cartoonist for over twenty years. His art has appeared in books, magazines, and on television, but he's best known for his work with comic books. In 1998, he began writing and illustrating the comic book *Age of Bronze*, a grand retelling of the Trojan War. *Age of Bronze* draws from Homer's classic account of war in Troy, *The Iliad*, but it also makes extensive use of the archaeological research conducted in Anatolia over the last hundred years. Eric Shanower's art is a rich and detailed visualization of past peoples. It has earned him two separate Eisner Awards, the highest honor in the comic book industry. It has also attracted the attention of professional archaeologists and classical scholars. Eric Shanower's work is a conduit into how we picture the past and the ways in which archaeology informs a wider audience. In the fall of 2005, after twenty-one issues and two serialized volumes into an expected set of seven (Shanower 2001, 2004), the artist explained the impetus for *Age of Bronze* and how archaeology has served his art.

TROY LOVATA: *What set you to work on a retelling of the Trojan War?*

ERIC SHANOWER: I often listen to audio books while I'm working. In the early 1990s, I listened to the book *The March of Folly: From Troy to Vietnam* by Barbara Tuchman (1985). The chapter on the Trojan War and the folly of the Trojans bringing the wooden horse into their city struck me. I was intrigued by the idea that the Trojan War story had been told over and over again in many versions through the centuries. I thought that a new version of the Trojan War that collected all the versions of the story while reconciling inconsistencies and set in the correct period of the Aegean Late Bronze Age would make a great comic book.

At first, the project seemed overwhelming. I scribbled a couple notes and tucked the idea away in my ideas file, figuring that the chances I'd ever do anything with it were as good as the chances I wouldn't. I had other projects I hoped to accomplish first. But gradually those other projects fell aside for one reason or another and the idea of retelling the Trojan War kept returning to the forefront of my mind. So I gave in and began researching the project.

**Figure 5.4
Odysseus and
Agamemnon Get
Their Ships**

Eric Shanower's
retelling of The Iliad
in comic-book form
required more than
just a translation
from one literary
genre to another. It
had to show how
specific objects and
particular characters
might have looked.
This meant that
the artist had to
find a balance
between literature,
archaeology, and
art. From Age of
Bronze, Volume 1:
A Thousand Ships.
Reproduced courtesy
of the artist.

T.L.: *Before you began Age of Bronze did you have any formal or informal experiences with archaeology—either as an adult or a youngster?*

E.S.: I think the first time I was exposed to the idea of archaeology was in learning about dinosaurs—that's probably pretty common for most kids in the United States. Of course, I've been to various museums both in North America and Europe and viewed artifacts from across time and place. I've been to famous sites such as the Athenian Acropolis, Stonehenge, and Williamsburg, to name a few. In 1977, I saw the King Tut exhibit that toured the U.S. and that inspired a fascination for ancient Egypt. Just before I began researching *Age of*

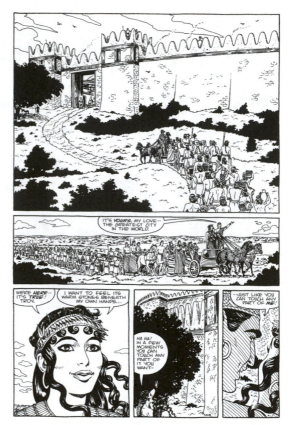

Figure 5.5 Helen Enters Troy

Eric Shanower portrays a scene of Paris introducing Helen, his new wife, to the city of Troy. From Age of Bronze, Volume 2: Sacrifice. Reproduced courtesy of the artist.

Bronze, I'd been doing research on ancient Egypt's 18th Dynasty for a comics project, but for various reasons, that project hasn't happened. For various comics projects, I've had to do research for costumes and settings of different times and cultures. So I had some familiarity with period research before I began *Age of Bronze*.

T.L.: *What kind of research into archaeology did you do when the comic book was starting? Has it changed now that you've put out more than twenty issues and been at this for several years?*

E.S.: In the beginning, I went to libraries. I looked at a lot of pictures in books and read a lot of information on Troy and the Mycenaean culture. Eventually, I had to include Hittite culture, too. As I noted, just before beginning *Age of Bronze* I'd been researching

Figure 5.6 Not just Writing, but Showing

A comic-book account of the Trojan War allows for the images to tell the story in ways that the written alone word cannot. From Eric Shanower's Age of Bronze, Volume 2: Sacrifice. Reproduced courtesy of the artist.

Ancient Egypt. One of the reasons that project stalled was that we have so much information from Ancient Egypt—it's really difficult to assimilate. We have much less from the Aegean Bronze Age. What a relief to find, for instance, photos of the Warrior Vase again and again in every book I looked at. I quickly realized I could handle the amount of research on the Trojan War. Not that it's been a completely smooth road. There are gaps in our knowledge, disagreements between sources, and different interpretations of the material. And there's always more material to absorb, but not the incredible Everest that we have from Ancient Egypt.

When I learned in 1995 that Troy was being excavated again, I was really excited. I immediately contacted the University of Cincinnati, the U.S. partner of the international archaeological team. The new excavations, which have been going on since 1988, have made some really exciting discoveries, and I'm glad and thankful to be able to incorporate them into *Age of Bronze*.

Also in the mid-1990s, I took night classes on the archaeology of Greece and the Near East (also on Egypt and Rome, but these were tangential to *Age of Bronze*). The research hasn't changed much since I first began it, except that I don't have to learn the basics anymore. Now I can usually recognize locations in Troy and Mycenae in photographs. I know what Linear B is. At this point, it's more refining the details than painting in the broad strokes. But still, when I'm drawing, for instance, a chariot, I have to go back to the primary research and refamiliarize myself with the differences between a Mycenaean chariot and a Hittite one.

T.L.: *Apart from illustrating the story of the Trojan War, you're probably best known for work based on L. Frank Baum's Wizard of Oz. Any contrasts or connections between drawing what could be described as the magical, Oz, and the mythical, Troy?*

E.S.: I've been an Oz fan since I was a child, so I've been steeping in that phenomenon for a long time. Not till I was an adult did I decide to learn about the Trojan War, both the literary aspect and the archaeological aspect, and then specifically for *Age of Bronze*; my interest didn't grow out of a previous enthusiasm as did my Oz comics, writing, and illustration.

One similarity between these areas—Oz and the Trojan War—is that I needed to be as familiar with the Trojan War as I was with Oz. I'd been reading the Oz books since childhood and had memorized the most obscure details. I could recite passages of dialogue from the *Wizard of Oz* movie. I'd like to say that I have as encyclopedic a knowledge of the Trojan War as I did for Oz, but while working on *Age of Bronze* I still have to go look things up and I don't always know exactly where to go to find the information.

T.L.: *Your readers have written you, initiating discussions about what specifically happened in the past and you seem to have developed a pretty friendly relationship with professional archaeologists—for instance, you've been invited to speak at archaeology conferences. How do you react to being considered an expert about what happened in the past?*

E.S.: First and foremost I'm a cartoonist. I'm not an expert in history or archaeology. I try to make that clear to those who might mistake me for such. The knowledge that I've gathered about the Trojan War—both literary and archaeological—is in support of *Age of Bronze*. The idea for the comic came first; the comic didn't grow from a body of knowledge I already had. If, in the process of my research, I've gained some degree of expertise, that's fine and I'm happy to share any knowledge or insight of my own. But I try always to defer to the real archaeologists and scholars.

One of my goals in *Age of Bronze* is to make it accessible to someone who has never heard either of Homer or of Heinrich Schliemann. But I really appreciate those readers who do know something about the background I'm drawing from. I think that incorporating the archaeological aspect into my retelling of the Trojan War can bring the general reader a greater appreciation, however small, for archaeology. At the same time, I hope *Age of Bronze* gives archaeology an interesting face to the general reader without pablumizing it. I definitely appreciate any approval for *Age of Bronze* it receives from archaeologists. And I'm grateful for all the positive response it's gotten from that quarter.

T.L.: *Gods and the supernatural are conspicuously absent from Age of Bronze. Likewise, even though this is a very iconic story, you present the characters with deep motives, multi-dimensional lives and fully human personalities. How concerned are you with accuracy—in the story you tell, in the objects people use, in what motivates these people from the past?*

E.S.: I've removed the gods in my version of the story in order to emphasize the human aspect. One of the most fascinating things about the project is finding motivations for the characters' actions. Sometimes they do the most heinous things. For instance, Agamemnon lets his daughter be slaughtered in front of him. I'm interested in showing how people—not just people in an ancient story, but by inference everyday people all around you—can arrive at decisions like this.

But I have to stay within the framework I've been given. I'm not creating the story of the Trojan War, but re-creating it. The entire thing was lying around in many pieces before I got the idea for *Age of Bronze*. My responsibility is to make the actions of the characters seem possible and plausible within a context that's already established. Of course, I decide how the established pieces will fit together in my version. I write the dialogue, determine the pacing, the movement of scenes, and draw the actions and reactions of the characters. But I don't think it would be fair to add major new elements I've created myself. Sometimes I have to tread carefully. For instance, in telling Cassandra's history—how she got to be the woman whose prophecies would never be believed—I gathered all the different versions of her story. In combining them and removing the supernatural elements, the idea of childhood sexual trauma became pretty clear. To a reader who has only a vague idea of the source material, this might seem like something I've added to the story, but when I retrace the source material, the result I came up with seems obvious all over again to me.

So, in that case I feel I was on safe ground from the viewpoint of the literary tradition. Was I on safe ground from the archaeological viewpoint? Would the Trojan culture of the thirteenth-century BCE produce the reaction I've given to Cassandra? That's a good question for which I have no firm answer. Societal standards and pressures are the sort of things that disappear with time, they're difficult to recover with archaeology. Written records might help, but we have only one example of writing from Late Bronze Age Troy, a short religious inscription. I think that in *Age of Bronze* Cassandra acts and reacts in a recognizably human manner, so, since archaeology doesn't provide much foundation in this case, human nature in conjunction with the literary tradition is what I relied on.

Accuracy in the objects people use, as well as in their dress and in the settings around them, is also very important to me. My ideal is always to use an archaeological source when drawing such things. Sometimes I easily find what I need—weapons, architecture—these are well documented both by physical remains and in drawings the people of the time have left for us. Sometimes I can't find what I need in either the Mycenaean or Hittite research and have to look a little farther afield. For instance, I've drawn musical instruments from Ancient Egypt. Other times I have to extrapolate. One example of that is in the buildings on top of the Trojan citadel, which was shorn off in antiquity. I've had to look at architecture from Hattusas and other Hittite sites to create what I hope are plausible reconstructions of Priam's palace and Trojan temples.

T.L.: *Are you ever concerned about giving modern-day personalities and drives to people from antiquity or do you believe that there are essential human traits that transcend time and place?*

E.S.: Both. I'm concerned about giving modern day personalities and drives to people from antiquity, and I also believe that there are essential human traits that transcend time and place. One of the reasons, I think, that the story of the Trojan War has survived the centuries is that the actions and desires of the characters are recognizably human. The big ideas of love, pride, anger, fear, greed, lust, and shame are constant in the human experience as a whole. It's the day-to-day societal norms and cultural expectations that change. I certainly try to adhere to what we know of the culture of the Late Bronze Age Aegean world, but societal norms and cultural expectations disappear. Archaeology has a difficult time reconstructing this sort of thing, and even when there's archaeological evidence, it's hotly debated. Actually the literary tradition offers more to be relied upon in my case, since I'm re-creating a story from Greek mythology. I don't have to justify the actions of the characters in a wider context; I just need to make sure their actions seem authentic within the story I'm telling.

There are conflicts, though, among the different sources of my story. One example is the story of the Trojan prince Troilus. Homer mentions Troilus once in the *Iliad*, and from pottery art and later literary snippets we have a pretty good idea of Troilus's death at Achilles hands. But Troilus's story expanded immensely in the European middle ages, notably in Boccaccio's *Il Filostrato*, in Chaucer's *Troilus and Criseyde*, and into the Renaissance in Shakespeare's *Troilus and Cressida*. All these later Troilus works were influenced by the cultures of their times and places. So one of my tasks is to distill what's universal from the tradition of courtly love of the European middle ages and combine it with what we know of the culture of the Late Bronze Age Aegean world while remaining within the limits of the story of the Trojan War as a whole.

One of the most enjoyable parts of *Age of Bronze* is reconciling the different versions of the Trojan War story. While I strive for authenticity in my use of archaeological evidence, when it comes to the story itself, I certainly have some leeway. *Age of Bronze* is historical fiction, after all. Archaeology may not be able to tell us how a character would have reacted in a certain situation during the thirteen-century BCE, but my job as a storyteller is to make the reader believe that the character had little choice but to act that way.

I do have to take some care with dialogue. I can't have the characters use words from the Christian tradition—"damn" and "hell" are unquestionably out. And I try to keep contemporary slang to a minimum—I restrict the little I allow to the Trojan teenage boys. I wanted to use the word "romantic" at one point, but wasn't sure it was valid, since Rome wasn't established in the thirteenth-century BCE—in fact, in the literary tradition of the Trojan War, Rome is sort of a new Troy, indirectly founded by Aeneas. In the end, however, I used "romantic" because I decided that the characters weren't speaking English anyway, so "romantic" was my English translation of the (probably) Luwian word spoken by the character.

T.L.: *Your art bridges Greek mythology, literature, and archaeology. How do you find a balance between them? How do you judge which is telling an accurate story?*

E.S.: I don't have any hard rules about balancing between mythology/literature and archaeology. But I do have a guideline. Generally I use the mythology and literature in the story and the archaeology in the art. This is why, for instance, my version of Achilles is dark-haired. Homer gives him golden hair in the *Iliad*, but I have yet to see a Mycenaean drawing of someone with any color of hair but dark. So for Achilles' hair, archaeology wins. But it's a guideline, not a rule, so I can't claim perfect consistency. Homer gives Menelaus red hair, and my Menelaus has red hair, too, taken from the literary tradition. The reason was not because I've seen a Mycenaean drawing of a redhead, but because I wanted to distinguish the character from Agamemnon, since I've given these two brothers similar features.

I will not draw objects in *Age of Bronze* that I know to be anachronistic. I give myself a little leeway within the Late Bronze Age period. I confess that I don't stick strictly to Late Helladic IIIb. I will draw objects from earlier, say the fifteenth-century BCE, and even from a little later—but not much later. I stop before the Protogeometric period. I'm glad when I find ways to use archaeology to reinforce what I derive from the literary sources. The traditional Trojan War has no references to the Sea Peoples, but I definitely tried to let Paris' roving before he returned to Troy with Helen echo the movement of the Sea

Peoples at the end of the Bronze Age. I even made the men watching on the shore of Mysia aware of a lot of piratical raids. I intended that as a reference to the Sea Peoples.

While I certainly have respect for archaeology and I hope that I don't misuse or misconstrue it, in the end, all my efforts go toward telling the story of the Trojan War. I'm not sure there's a specifically "accurate" way. *Age of Bronze* is historical fiction, not a textbook. Another cartoonist would probably do it differently. My judgment in using and combining elements is governed by telling the story in the manner I think most valid. In the middle of working it's sometimes difficult to know whether I'm telling the story the best way, but I do the best I can.

T.L.: *Since you're both the author and the illustrator of Age of Bronze you have experience in presenting the past both visually and through text. Do you see any significant difference between deciding what characters say or do versus how they are visually portrayed?*

E.S.: It's really easy to write a panel description that says a character shoots an arrow from a bow. But when I sit down to draw it. I have to draw that bow. As far as I know we have no Mycenaean bows. We have Mycenaean pictures of bows, but those are frustratingly lacking in detail. So I start with only a little evidence and reconstruct from there.

Sometimes the archaeology informs the artwork in ways I didn't suspect at the beginning. For instance, there's a scene at Mycenae in which Telephus threatens to harm the baby Orestes. In the literary tradition, this takes place before an altar in some versions and by a hearth in other versions. In fact, the altar and the hearth may be one and the same, so at first I planned to set the scene before the central circular hearth in the throne room of Mycenae. But in going over the archaeological information, I found that there was the remnant of what appears to be an altar in the courtyard just outside the main megaron at Mycenae. So because archaeology provided both a hearth and an altar, I changed my idea and wrote the scene to let the action begin at the central hearth inside and move to the small altar outside. That movement was completely dictated by my effort to make my understanding of the archaeological evidence mesh with the literary evidence.

But comics is a synthesis of words and pictures, so for the most part what the characters say and do and what they look like are so closely connected that it's not really productive to think about them separately.

T.L.: *Have any professional archaeologists found faults with or given particular praise to your work?*

E.S.: Professional archaeologists have both found fault and given praise to *Age of Bronze*. I gratefully accept the praise. With faults of archaeological nature, I try to check my sources and research and decide whether I agree. Sometimes it's clear I've made the wrong choice, as in, for instance, a costume detail or the period of some pottery I've drawn. I try to do better from then on. But sometimes the choice I've made is debatable. How low in the water would Mycenaean ships float? What did the heads of the animals on Mycenae's lion gate look like? Difficult questions. But due to the nature of *Age of Bronze*, I've got to make definite choices because I've got drawings to finish. Not everyone will agree with my choices. Not all archaeologists agree with each other. I do the best I can.

Sometimes archaeologists have had opinions on things in *Age of Bronze* that aren't archaeological in nature. For instance, I received an objection to the scene early in the story in which Paris and Oenone are French kissing, and I was questioned about my inclusion of Pleisthenes, the infant son of Helen and Menelaus. But these are story matters, not archaeologically based, and I'm not sure professional archaeologists are necessarily more qualified than I am to judge story matters.

Still, the archaeology of Greece has long been intertwined with Greek mythology. To a large extent, it's been inspired by Greek mythology. So archaeologists of the Late Bronze Age Aegean tend to know a lot about the literary tradition. However, archaeologists tend to be far more enthusiastic about *Age of Bronze* than classicists are. Classicists often seem offended that I'm not adhering strictly to Homer. It seems difficult for them to accept that I'm drawing from the entire range of the Trojan War literary and artistic tradition. Classicists are the ones who give me negative reactions—classicists and those who want more fight scenes.

Interview Number Three:
Digging, Sorting, and Displaying

Mark Dion is a renowned American artist whose work has been on exhibit internationally since 1985. His art is built from both practice and presentation. It includes the systematic collection of materials—sometimes making use of entire crews of technicians, laboratory staff, and curators—and the arrangement of artifacts into cabinets of wonder and detailed displays. Archaeology has played a substantial role in his art. These include: the *History Trash Dig* (1995) and *History Trash Scan* (1996) of urban detritus in Switzerland and Italy,

Figure 5.7 A Cabinet of Wonders

An interactive display of artifacts from Mark Dion's History Trash Dig, 1997. Reproduced courtesy of the artist.

the dredging work of *Raiding Neptune's Vault* (displayed at the Venice Biennale in 1997), the collection of riverside artifacts for the *Tate Thames Dig* (commissioned by the Tate Modern in London, 1999), *The New England Digs* (for the Fuller Museum of Art, Massachusetts in 2001), and his recent work (2004–2005) with *Rescue Archaeology* for the Museum of Modern Art in New York City, in which he collected artifacts in an area of the museum under reconstruction. Mark Dion has also specifically engaged archaeologists themselves, with Professor Colin Renfrew of the University of Cambridge contributing to one of his books (Dion and Coles 1999) and with the artist himself writing a chapter for the volume *Material Engagements* (Brodie and Hills 2004) from the McDonald Institute for Archaeological Research. In November 2005, Mark Dion spoke about his art and how he makes use of archaeology.

Figure 5.8 Dressed to Collect

The artist in full artifact-hunting regalia—from "Mark Dion Beachcombing on London's Foreshore," the Tate Thames Dig, Site I, 1999. Photograph by Andrew Cross, reproduced courtesy of Mark Dion.

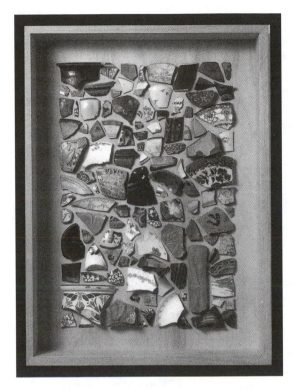

Figure 5.9 Artifacts on Display

"Loot 2," from Mark Dion's project Raiding Neptune's Vault, 1997/1998. The artist has chosen to display objects in ways that are artistically, not necessarily archaeologically, meaningful. Reproduced courtesy of Mark Dion.

TROY LOVATA: *What was your first foray into using archaeology in your art?*

MARK DION: I had an unusual situation in which a lot of my work was about the representation of nature. I found that, after awhile, at every exhibition I was being asked about art and ecology, art and nature, art and animals. After a time, I realized that by letting myself be classified I was really limiting myself. So I needed a way ahead and a way to get the hounds off my trail. I wanted to take on another field, another discipline, than zoology. Archaeology in some way uses my methodology of gathering and of the kind of practice I'd done with zoology. I could apply what I had done with zoology to something else that I had a personal interest in and a personal—an amateur—passion for. I got into archaeology as way of moving ahead in my work, but also moving to the side as well.

The first project I did was in Fribourg, Switzerland, where I had two different projects in two different galleries. One was an investigation of the microfauna living in a square meter of meadow. And in the other I had dug out an amount of material from a gorge that had been occupied for hundreds of years. So I took as much of that material as I could move into the gallery in one day. I went back into the gallery and proceeded to remove all the material culture from it. It was significant that I chose that location because the process of erosion had destroyed the context and all the stuff was sort of naturally mixed together. So archaeology was a way to focus on material culture and shift away from taxonomy.

T.L.: *Did you have much background in archaeology to guide you? Did you take any courses or have even an informal background?*

M.D.: I have an informal background—from visiting digs during excavation to visiting archaeological sites after excavation. One of my friend's mother is one of the archaeologists for the city of New York. So I'd spent a lot of time talking to her and visiting sites that she had worked on. I've kind of had a real amateur interest rather than a real academic one. I have friends that are amateurs that have sites that they've excavated—in Britain, for example. I've got to be able to visit them while they were working. I've seen quite a few different kinds of sites, even Native American sites and urban sites.

I grew up in New England, where one runs across both Native American and colonial things all the time. I guess a part of my fascination comes from wandering around New England and finding old foundations and bottle dumps. And I've always had a fascination with graveyards. So a lot of this comes, very much like my interest in the natural world, from experiences that were really fostered in childhood.

T.L.: *Do you find a link between the samples you're collecting when dealing with the natural world and the artifacts related to archaeology? Or does something stand out when you're dealing with culturally derived artifacts?*

M.D.: I think they are remarkably different. For me, what I've been interested in about the cultural artifacts, such as my work in European sites, is always trying to work on sites where the context has been destroyed for one reason or another. I'm interested in sites where things are quite mixed up. Part of me wants to create a microcosmic impression of what happens when I go to a European city. In a city like Fribourg, Switzerland, you might have houses from the thirteenth century that might be next to a cathedral and that might be next to a nineteenth-century hotel that has a new McDonald's in the basement. This is a kind of condensation of history that you can witness—almost simultaneity. That is very much what I try to encapsulate in my archaeological projects.

I think that my projects, wherever they are, are really motivated by a sense of awe with time. There's a sense of awe and of the marvelous when dealing with something so old. There's a historical depth that I might feel some kind of continuity to. That sense of continuity is a really important thing in all the projects that I do. I really want my projects to function in such a way that you get a sense of us as part of continuum of time and not as us as a pinnacle of time. This is in contrast to how an awful lot of people think of history; that everything is leading up to us as opposed to thinking about the continuity. That's one reason I used the river [in the Thames project] as a metaphor in some way. I used that notion of something that you step into that is coming before and coming after and that you're a moment in.

I think that an important part of my work is having some sort of inclusive element. I think things might be different if I worked with sites that have a greater depth—like in the Mediterranean or the Middle East or China. Those sorts of sites have had established civilizations for so long a time and have a very different kind of cultural tradition for me. I really do think that, as other people have said, that the past is a foreign country and that the past is a really difficult thing to try to contextualize. It's really difficult to try to image the consciousness of people living before you and I think that the further back you go the more difficult it is to find a kind of empathy with them.

T.L.: *When you mention the idea of being inclusive, this brings up the fact that your art involves more than just you—it often involves whole teams of people. Do you bring in these other people in order to make your work more approachable?*

M.D.: Absolutely. Sometimes the volunteers serve as an encapsulation of the goals the project. For instance, when I was working in London on the Thames project I had a set of volunteers and they had to be either under seventeen or over sixty-five—either teenagers or pensioners. The way that they related to each other is very much how I imagined the project conceptually. The teenagers had this sense of the "olden days." The "olden days" was basically everything from the Romans to the Beatles. Whereas some of the pensioners had lived through the Second World War. They had a different sense of the objects that we were finding. The teenagers would discover something and say, "Oh, oh! I found a bottle from the olden days!" They'd pick it up and then one of the pensioners would say, "Oh, that's not from the olden days, that's a bottle of Peck's toothpaste and that used to come in the ration boxes we got in the subways during the bombings of London." That suddenly made that object real in some sense for these kids and it took it out of this kind of mysterious historical realm that constituted the "olden days" for them.

In some ways, this is how I want all my projects to function. I want people to go through the material and suddenly find for themselves something that they recognize as part of their history and as part of their material culture—not as part of something that's distanced from them.

T.L.: *Critics note that you're neither categorizing nor displaying artifacts in the ways that an academic archaeologist would. What are you trying to do when you catalog and categorize?*

M.D.: I think that these kinds of artifacts are meaningful in a lot of different ways. I think they're aesthetically meaningful for instance. I try to have different categories and have the categories work where they're in competition with each other. In some of my display you can open one drawer and things are organized by color. In another drawer things are organized by utility. Open another drawer and things are organized by shape or physical similarity. So the minute you open them you try to image what are establishing these systems. Some of these systems use very childlike categories, very basic things, and some of them are more sophisticated. Some of them are categories based on the mixing of the natural and the artificial worlds—things like barnacles attached to a glass bottle or where oxidation has made metal unrecognizable.

I like the way in which my displays are like curiosity cabinets in which natural objects were embellished with carving or inlaid or placed in elaborate mounts. The mixing of the natural and the artificial doesn't seem as contradictory as it does now. So I'm sort of geared toward those objects which are hybrids.

This is also a link with my interest in the evolution of museums. I'm trying to trace back how the museums we recognize today developed through a process of learning about society and the Enlightenment. How they come from a Renaissance moment where treasures come out from the Medieval idea of a treasure trove, where you hide your treasures and fortify them. The Renaissance model is one where you display your treasures. They're the invention of bling-bling. That's a really interesting moment in the evolution of the museum and how we get to where we are now. That's something I've thought a lot about in my work and that's really shaped the direction of some of these projects.

T.L.: *You've been displayed in art museums. Is there something fundamentally different in that compared to a natural history museum or an archaeology museum?*

M.D.: This is something I ask myself about all the time. We have a situation in which the art is the hybrid overlap. In New York City we have the Natural History Museum on one side of the park [Central Park] and we have the Met [Metropolitan Museum of Art] on the other side of the park. Some people's culture gets to be natural history and some people's culture gets to be fine art. Sometimes it's the exact same things that can be found on different sides of the park, but they're radically recontextualized. I think the same is true of most archaeology. You know, some archaeology falls under the rubric of natural history. In our American tradition, very often Native American culture is framed in that way. I think that you can look at that, obviously, in the terms of the history of art. How do you classify the Egyptian and Roman galleries in the Metropolitan? Is that not archaeology?

I think that this is an interesting question. I think that these lines are very blurry in some ways. I'm interested, for my projects, in how that works in a contemporary sense. I can look at my displays, like my cabinets, and the discourse they produce is very lively and very engaging. People are opening drawers, interacting with objects, interacting with each other. They're laughing. They're very engaged. If I put it in an archaeology museum I just don't see that happening as an activity amongst the public.

That's also the explanation for why archaeologists can get be interested what I do. Clearly they know that this is not a certain archaeological practice under a certain set of rules. But, at the same time, they are very engaged with this type of thing because I seem to be able to bridge a gap between what they do and a broader public that they have a hard time bridging.

T.L.: *How have archaeologists perceived your work? What's the feedback been like?*

M.D.: I think that there's a wide range of things. There are some people that obviously think that it's dangerous. That it's degrading—that I'm removing artifacts without proper procedure. This is something that comes from what I think of as a much more pragmatic school of archaeology, which is what you have here in the United States.

I think that in Europe it's generally been treated in a more theoretical way. They seem to recognize that I'm always using sites that are already somehow context-polluted. I try never to work in a place that disturbs context. I think they find my work more as a kind of theoretical challenge. They think of it as a way of looking at their way of doing things and using it as critical foil in a nonthreatening way. They understand that there's a degree of humor, of irony and parody, that as scientists it's really difficult for them to have access to and use. They are really interested in the critique of the institution of archaeology. They are really interested in a critique which is much more about the display methods and the didactic forms. My pieces are less critical toward archaeology itself than toward the means with which archaeology is translated for the general public. In other words, more critical not of the back rooms of a museum, but more critical of what archaeologists do in the exhibit part of the museum.

One thing—and I think that this is a very important thing when it comes to thinking about science in general—is that it's quite often not the scientists who speak with certitude and are so prone to making definitive claims. Speaking with a certain kind of authority, like a journalist would, is something that a scientist would be very cautious of.

T.L.: *Do you ever face a situation in which you're assumed to be the author-ity and you need to back off? Perhaps some of your volunteers come to you wanting to be told exactly what to do or told exactly what an object that they've uncovered is?*

M.D.: Absolutely. There's almost three phases to these projects. There's the dig itself. For the dig, I think the volunteers are primary audi-ence. The people who are giving of themselves to the project are really a small audience—for the New England digs that may have been a hundred people. That's really the primary audience for this part of the work—even though it's public, it's not advertised. It's not really perfor-mance in the sense of having a traditional audience to perform for.

The second part is the cleaning of the material and the sorting of it. And that is very public and is very dynamic. That's the point the where we have a really interesting relationship with the audience because they have access to us. It's really interesting to see how dif-ficult it can be for audience members who come up, pick up a pottery sherd and say, "What is this?" And we say, "We don't know."

People often ask me, "Do you organize these things, do you label these things?" Of course, with the Thames project, we put every sin-gle thing out there and had them identify it...well, as much as they could. I'm not doing that. That's what they do. That's one of the big-gest differences in terms of my projects and archaeology. In one of my other projects I photographed insects. I closed the museum and found all these insects and photographed them. I photographed them and sprayed them without scale and without names. And that's the way an entomologist would never do things!

T.L.: *So that's the step that's not entomology and, in other works, this is the step that's not archaeology?*

M.D.: Exactly. I'm really trying to do that. That's very awkward and really frustrating for the public. They want something different. In this second stage, the public very much sees this like the *Antiques Roadshow* [television program]. They want to know what's the oldest thing you've found and what's the most valuable thing you've found.

I think that this engagement with the public is a social one. It's not a very informative one in the sense that people can come and be told what something actually is. By the end of our time in London, we had people bring us things that they had found. They brought us things to identify. And when you don't deliver, that's very disconcerting for them.

The third stage is the actual display of the sorted material itself. In this stage, there is no interaction. There is no talking back. This isn't the hardest stage for me. I'm trying to create a situation that exists without me watching over them. The work is a kind of interpretation in some sense. The idea that they may leave with more questions than they came in with is intriguing to me. That's what I'm wanting. That's what I'm eager about.

T.L.: *You seem to have had a view into the inner workings of archaeology. Has this insight affected your work or changed how you do things?*

M.D.: It's given me a better appreciation of how different what I do is from the contemporary practice of archaeology. What's funny to me is that, for many people, what I do looks more and seems more like archaeology than the archaeology I've seen practiced. When I see archaeologists looking at pollen samples under a scanning electron microscope or things like that, it doesn't seem part of the tradition or the romance of archaeology. Perhaps my work seems, superficially at least, to have a link. What I'm doing looks more like archaeology to a general viewer.

One of the interesting things about knowing about what goes on behind the scenes of archaeology is really seeing how different it is. I would certainly never claim in any way to be an archaeologist and understand the complexity behind it.

T.L.: *Nonetheless, you seem to have enough understanding of archaeology to build a sheen of what the public thinks you need to be if you're doing archaeology—the way you should dress or the tools you use.*

M.D.: I'm always impressed by the power of a uniform and the power of a costume. If I put on the right vest and I carry the right clipboard and I have the right hard hat, then it seems like I can pass myself off as almost anything. My passing, for most people, looks like archaeology and feels like archaeology. I'm dabbling with a lot of the same tools. To them it's archaeology.

For me it becomes interesting to elaborate this in the final parts of my projects. That's why I go out of my way with the material culture I've gathered to think, "OK, how can I show you in a way that an archaeologist wouldn't?" "What can I make out of this that's different from you, as an archaeologist, would make out of this?" And I'm not talking about what I can make out of this in a way someone like Picasso would make. I'm talking about creating an information structure or creating some kind of information flow that is different from the narrative, of development of technology or the refinement of an object, which you would find in archaeology.

References and Further Reading

Benjamin, W.
1969   *Illuminations*. Translated by H. Zohn. Schoken Books, New York.

Brodie, N. and C. Hills
2004   *Material Engagements*. McDonald Institute Monographs, Cambridge, England.

Copper, M.C. and E.B. Shoedsack
1933   *King Kong*. Universal Studios, Hollywood, California.

DeMille. C.B.
1956   *The Ten Commandments*. Paramount Pictures, Hollywood, California.

Dion, M. and A. Coles
·1999   *Archaeology*. Black Dog Publishing, Ltd., London.

James, S.
1997   Drawing Inferences: Visual Reconstruction in Theory and Practice. In *The Cultural Life of Images*. B. Molyneaux, editor. Routledge, London.

Lovata, T.
2005   Shovel Bum—The Life Archaeologic. In *Underground!: The Disinformation Guide to Ancient Civilizations, Astonishing Archaeology and Hidden History*. P. Peet, editor. The Disinformation Company, Ltd., New York.

Lumet, S.
1976   *Network*. MGM, Hollywood, California.

Moser, S.
1998   *Ancestral Images: The Iconography of Human Origins*. Cornell University Press, Ithaca, New York.

Shanower, E.
2001   *Age of Bronze, Volume One: A Thousand ships*. Image Comics, Orange, California.

2004   *Age of Bronze, Volume Two: Sacrifice*. Image Comics, Orange, California.

Tuchman, B.
1985   *The March of Folly: From Troy to Vietnam*. Ballantine Books, New York.

Critical Questions and Exercises

1. Artists Adam Horowitz, Eric Shanower, and Mark Dion use different media and come from different backgrounds. Yet, each has ended up using archaeology in their work. Review their responses to similar questions and search for similarities in what drove them to archaeology. This requires you to determine how they define archaeology—an import step in understanding the relationship between the professional and public spheres of the discipline. Is archaeology a set of artifacts? Is it a series of stories about the past? Or is it a certain way of acting, dressing, and looking at the world? What does each artist say about these different aspects of archaeology?

2. Understanding the attraction of the archaeology to these three artists also lets you consider how they approach the idea of authenticity in their work. Examine the extents to which they feel they need to accurately portray the archaeological record. Explore whether their art depends on authenticity to be successful. Do they expect the people who view their work to want or need a particular level or kind of authenticity? Why or why not might this be the case?

3. Study how an artist's view of authenticity might differ from an archaeologist's even though, as mentioned in the beginning of this book, both art and archaeology reference the work of Walter Benjamin (1969). This chapter presented the artists' own thoughts on the subject. Do some research into the archaeologists who also create art and use their observations as comparative perspectives. Good places to start include: the writings of Simon James, whose essay "Drawing Inferences: Visual Reconstruction in Theory and Practice" is found in the book *The Cultural Life of Images* (1997), works by and about John Gurche, whose paintings of paleo-humans have been featured in major museums and magazines such as *National Geographic*, and the newsletters, journals, and books published by the Association of Archaeological Illustrators and Surveyors—including their extensive website and their periodical *Graphic Archaeology*.

4. These interviews note that several archaeologists have purposely engaged with artists Eric Shanower and Mark Dion. Review the ways in which each has been contacted by and worked with professional scholars, researchers, and academics. Then review your responses to the previous question about archaeologists who also try their hand at art. What specifically about art and artists might attract the interest of archaeologists? Does it somehow balance against the idea that archaeology is science based (as discussed in Chapter 1)? Is the attraction related to the end product—pieces of art—or to the abilities of an artist to think, act, or work in ways different from many professional archaeologists?

Chapter 6

Megalithomania! Archaeology at Play

Sometimes archaeology is simply too much fun to ignore. It draws you in and its sheer presence pushes aside seemingly serious questions of provenance and provability. Defining things as authentic, original, or accurate may no longer matter when you come across an opportunity for an unchecked physical experience with the archaeological record.

Re-Creations and Replicas of Megaliths

Megaliths are massive stones that mark a human presence on the landscape. Some are individual rocks propped up for greater visibility. Others are piles or stacks of large stones. Some megaliths are purposely arranged in series, circles, and alignments. Many have been carved into specific shapes, bored through, or adorned with images. They go by names like dolmen, menhirs, cairns, mounds, towers, trilithons, arches, pyramids, henges, crosses, and circles. Megaliths are found worldwide, but some of the most well-known and well-studied examples are in Europe. Most megaliths look quite old and appear very primitive—they are rock after all. Many are rough hewn in comparison to modern straight edges and sharp corners. Many megaliths are, in fact, quite old.

Megaliths, like Stonehenge in England, are arguably some of the most well-known archaeological sites in the world. Megaliths have long attracted the attention of both professional and amateur archaeologists alike, because they serve as such enduring monuments to past peoples and past ways of life. Their sheer size, their solid form, and what seems to be their ability to defy the ravages of time have piqued the interest of generations. Their age and scale never fail to bring up such questions as why so much work was put into their construction, how primitive tools and technologies could have formed and placed such massive stones, and what meaning lies behind their shapes and alignments. Megaliths, both their material manifestations and the ideas they entail, have attracted enormous attention. Pop musician and connoisseur of megaliths Julian Cope (1992) poetically notes as much in his catchy proclamation:

> Everywhere Megaliths Everywhere
> I see stone circles everywhere…
>
> …I've got Avebury on the brain
> And I'm on Salisbury Plain
>
> Ancient History—I can't contain ya
> I got Megalithomania!

It should be no surprise that megaliths are so popular that they have been copied. People have long built replicas, imitations, and re-creations of megaliths and megalithic sites. The phenomenon is neither new nor a short-term fad. Archaeologist Glyn Daniels (1959) noted that mock megaliths in the country of England alone have at least a three-hundred-year history. They stretch from a dolmen in the Cotswolds erected in the early eighteenth century, to the nineteenth-century re-creation of Stonehenge near Masham in Yorkshire, to the mid-twentieth-century-megalithic-panel façade of Cambridge University's Chemistry Laboratory. Many of these replicas and re-creations can be understood as participation in—and celebration of—a people's, region's, or nation's heritage. John Michell (1982:156) observed that interest in megaliths is at least partly explained by the fact that, "every culture is umbilically linked with its native countryside."

However, there are also replicas built by individuals who don't literally see themselves as descendants of ancient megalithic peoples. There are replicas erected in places in which no known prehistoric examples have been found. Likewise, there are replicas constructed of materials other than stone. There are sites that proudly display their inaccuracies and incongruities. There are sites that advertise the fact that, although they look like ancient megaliths, they are definitely not so. These examples require more explanation than just geographic or ancestral proximity to ancient originals. These unabashedly mock megaliths, the reasons for their existence, and the ways in which they function, all warrant deeper scrutiny. Their very presence informs us as to how audiences interact with the past and how much people might value authenticity versus other qualities and other experiences.

Figure 6.1 Stonehenge II
A view of Stonehenge II, looking to the north. The site, located outside Hunt, Texas, is an obviously out-of-place and inauthentic construction.

Megaliths, Deep in the Heart of Texas

Stonehenge II is the proper name for a monumental re-creation of the famous megalithic circle of England's Salisbury Plain flanked two Easter Island Heads (properly known as Rapa Nui moai) on the southern edge of the Texas Hill Country (figure 6.1). Stonehenge II lies on a privately owned, ten-acre plot near the hamlet of Hunt—about 150 kilometers southwest of Austin, the Texas state capitol. The site is approximately 8,000 kilometers from England and over 5,000 kilometers from the shores of Easter Island. Stonehenge II is adjacent to Texas State Highway 39 and is clearly visible to passing motorists. Cars can be found pulling over here nearly every day of the year. Their occupants are seen making their way across the road and through a fence (figure 6.2). Inside the fence, at approximately 90% original size, lies a circle of megaliths framed a few hundred meters to the west and southwest by the pair of anthropomorphic moai.

Figure 6.2 Shadows of the Past

A close-up of the concrete and chicken wire arches of Stonehenge II. The fence that surrounds the site and Texas State Highway 39, which arcs around the property, is visible in the background.

There are only two actual stones at the site—large slabs of limestone taken from the surrounding cliffs and laid inside the eighteen-meter diameter ring of trilithons (figure 6.3). The inner trilithons, the outside ring of the henge, and the moai are all hollow. They are fashioned from chicken wire forms stuccoed with concrete and fastened to the ground to form a permanent part of the landscape. Each structure simulates the effect of rock and shows their builder's careful attention to detail. These are not smoothed, form-set constructions with sharp angles and flat surfaces. Instead, relatively rough stucco surfaces and shallow, undulating waves mimic the niches, notches, and cut marks of hand-carved rock. The moai are detailed down to their nipples, nostrils, and navels. One wears a "hat" of weathered, red-stained concrete as a copy of the top knots on some Easter Island originals, as well as an allusion to the ten-gallon cowboy hat, Texas's most iconic form of haberdashery (figure 6.4). On the far side of the lawn, at the end of a long drive, sits a small ranch house—the former home of the mastermind behind this site.

Figure 6.3 Inside the Circle of Stonehenge II

There are only two true stones at the site: limestone blocks laid horizontally (approximately 220 cm in length) and vertically (approximately 150 cm in height) in a de facto altar.

Figure 6.4 One of Two Heads

Alfred Shepperd erected two Easter Island heads, more properly known as Rapa Nui moai, alongside his henge. Some examples from the Pacific island wear what archaeologists have labeled as top knots. They've become cowboy hats in a south Texas context.

How and Why Stonehenge II Was Built

Stonehenge II was the inspiration of a retired Texas rancher. Alfred Shepperd wanted to interact with passersby and share his experiences of the world outside his south Texas home. Various articles compiled on the Shepperd family website explain that, in the late 1980s, Alfred Shepperd received from neighbor Doug Hill a large limestone slab left over from patio construction (Shepperd 2001). Shepperd initially placed this single rock straight up in the middle of his lawn and carefully mowed around the area for all to see. But the retired rancher

Stonehenge America

Nearly a half century ago, archaeologist Glyn Daniels (1959) compiled a list of Stonehenge replicas from across the United Kingdom. Their variety highlights something of the attraction of the original. It should be of little surprise, then, considering the strength of such a draw, that Stonehenge II in Texas is but one of many Stonehenge replicas in North America. These U.S. examples were assembled for a number of different reasons and out of a variety of materials.

Some replicas are primarily references to the real and supposed astronomical alignments of the original. For example, the UMR Stonehenge is a fifty-foot diameter and thirteen-and-a-quarter-foot-high circle—approximately half the size of the one at Avebury—crafted out of 160 tons of granite. The site lies near the Mines and Metallurgy building on the campus of the University of Missouri at Rolla and was erected by the school on the summer solstice in 1984. Numerous astronomical observations can be made at different times of the year using the henge's structure as a base. The university is especially proud of what the site represents both technically and culturally. Others clearly agree as the UMR Stonehenge was honored with one of only ten Outstanding Engineering Achievement Awards given out by the National Society of Professional Engineers in 1984.

Other replicas may be astronomically aligned, but were built more with the intention of delivering a message or honoring a sacrifice instead of serving as guide to the heavens. The Georgia Guidestones are a trilithon-like structure on a high prominence in Elbert County, Georgia. The site was crafted under the direction of R. C. Christian, and its central cluster of nineteen-foot-tall interlocking megaliths was dedicated in March 1980. Interestingly, the structure is carved from granite mined at the same quarry that would later provide the raw materials for the UMR Stonehenge. A hole was bored through the center stone to allow people to find the North Star, but the Georgia Guidestones function mainly as a statement about how people should live. A plaque at the base declares "LET THESE BE A GUIDE-STONE TO AN AGE OF REASON," and the upright slabs are covered with directions in multiple languages—including English, Swahili, Sanskrit, Classical Greek, Babylonian Cuneiform, and Egyptian hieroglyphics—on how to live in harmony. The advice it offers includes suggestions to unite humanity with a single language; guide reproduction wisely; avoid petty and useless officials; use a world court to solve international conflicts; leave room for nature; and prize beauty, love, and truth.

A less esoteric honorary Stonehenge lies on a scenic overlook of the Columbia River in Maryhill, Washington. The imposing U.S. Stonehenge was built out of cast concrete by committed Quaker pacifist Sam Hill as a monument to the men from surrounding Klickitat County who died in World War One. The site was dedicated in 1918, which makes it the first monument to Americans lost in the war. But the henge itself wasn't completed for another dozen years—just before Hill himself died in 1931. Many people, including those at the local museum, claim that Hill was under the mistaken belief that the original Stonehenge in England was a sacrificial altar and thus chose the same form to remind us that humanity is still being sacrificed to the god of war. Today, the replica is part of an entire memorial complex that includes Sam Hill's own grave and other monuments to local men who perished in World War Two, the Korean War, and Viet Nam.

Adam Horowitz's Stonefridge/Fridgehenge on the outskirts of Santa Fe, New Mexico, is discussed in detail in Chapter 5 of this book. Like Horowitz, other artists and builders have also chosen discarded materials for their re-creations instead of using stone or concrete. In 1986, Canadian artist William Lishman erected Autohenge on a grassy knoll outside of Oshawa, Ontario. This full-size replica was built, appropriately enough of, from partially crushed automobiles. Although the site was a popular attraction—it even appeared on the cover of one of archaeologist Christopher Chippindale's books (1987)—it only stood for five years. Jim Reinder's Carhenge is located near Alliance, Nebraska, and was raised in honor of his father, who lived on a farm where the henge now stands. It is another circle constructed of discarded—but not crushed—automobiles. Carhenge was dedicated on the summer solstice in 1987 and still stands today. The site is made up of thirty-eight grey-painted cars and even includes a partially buried 1962 Cadillac as a heel stone. Carhenge is currently owned and managed by the nonprofit Friends of Carhenge, who have erected other car-based sculptures on the property. The site is a popular tourist attraction, plays host to annual solstice gatherings, and has been featured in a number of U.S. and international movies, music videos, and advertisements.

Finally, there have been several large-size U.S. henges built from lightweight materials that contrast with the stone original. This includes sites like the Belluz family's Mystical Strawhenge—a hay bay circle annually erected for paying visitors on the wagon tour of the family's farm outside Thunder Bay, Ontario—and Lisa Galli's Mudhenge. Galli's henge was a temporary set of faux-megaliths built in Nevada's Black Rock Desert in 1996 as part of the annual Burning Man festival. The large slabs themselves were made of wood, but they surrounded a pit of mud into which spectators were invited to wallow. Another interesting example of material contrast is Virginia's Foamhenge. Sculptor Mark Cline erected this grey-painted, lightweight, yet full-size styrofoam circle in the Blue Ridge Mountains in just a single day in March 2004. But the high speed and lightweight are countered by Cline's observation (quoted in Carlson 2006) that, "Styrofoam is nonbiodegrable, so Foamhenge might outlast Stonehenge."

was unhappy with the relative scale of his installation and its limited attraction to passing motorists. Over the next year, Shepperd enlisted Hill's help to erect a circle of European-looking megalithic arches around the original stone. Shepperd considered this his retirement hobby and, following a trip to Easter Island in the early 1990s, the two moai were added. Shepperd died in 1994, just before he could raise a large totem pole—inspired by Alaska travels—next to the heads and henges. Although this didn't happen, his family keeps the land, maintains and repairs the structures, and continues to allow visitors on site.

Stonehenge II is neither a park, a museum, nor a money-making attraction. There are no tour guides, brochures for visitors, nor billboards up the road announcing the site. Visitors are free to roam at will. Only a sense of courtesy, which is entailed in the knowledge that this is private property, restricts their movement. The curious are beckoned through a break in the fence by an extremely brief and only slightly informative sign spelling out the supposed mystery of the original Stonehenge (figure 6.5).

Figure 6.5 Stonehenge II Is Not Meant to Be Educational or Informative

A single sign provides a minimum of information about the Stonehenge II and its creators. It connects the site to the mystery of the English original. Instead of giving a meaningful explanation or context, it raises more questions than it answers.

None of Stonehenge II's use or reason for existence is readily explained to its visitors. There are brief mentions of the site in local tour guides—the moai even appear on one's cover—and the Shepperd family maintains a website that archives a few articles that appeared in the news stories and the national, rural newspaper *Capper's Weekly* (McLeod 1995; Shepperd 2001). But this place falls outside the traditional Texas tourist trail of the Alamo in San Antonio, Padre Island along the Gulf Coast, Dealey Plaza in Dallas, and NASA in Houston. Unlike those developed attractions, nothing is forced on the visitor to Stonehenge II. Here, tourists are left to their own devices to experience what they may. The visceral presence of the structures, the seemingly inherent mystery of megaliths alluded to in the site's signage, and the oddity of such a monument in this locale all evoke wonder.

Stonehenge II is a playful construction that defies qualms about its authenticity. The circular henge and abutting moai are not meant to fool passersby into believing they are seeing original, prehistoric artifacts. This is not a convincing reconstruction in terms of accuracy. Very few people who happen on Stonehenge II would believe they have been physically transported to England or Easter Island. Visitors know they're still in Texas and not the land of the originals. Once visitors get close in, they see the site is built primarily of concrete and not fashioned from authentic rock. Stonehenge II is not a case of an original having been lifted from its footings and moved to Texas for display. This place is both patently out of place and unoriginal.

Traditions of Recreation and Leisure Time

Although Stonehenge II doesn't depend on an appeal to accuracy, it still draws from the existence of the English and Rapa Nui megaliths that it resembles. Alfred Shepperd did not randomly decide to erect his own versions of the heads and henges. He was drawing on long and well-known traditions. He wanted visitors. So Shepperd built an attraction and built from traditions of attraction.

The history and existence of the original English Stonehenge is one of visitation. The site owes its eminence to the legions of tourists who came to experience the stones. Nowadays, Stonehenge functions primarily as the site for recreational activities. Archaeologist Barbara Bender (1998) notes that the site hosted 20,000 paying visitors in the 1920s, 180,000 in 1955, and over 670,000 in 1994. Bender (1998:123) recounts that, "on a hot Summer's day in the peak year of 1977, 7000 people arrived in the course of a day and there were two thousand visitors in one hour." Archaeologist Christopher Chippindale (1994) explains that concerns about how society should deal with the crush of visitors—they are accused of literally eroding the site away with their footsteps, hand prints, tire tracks, and collection of souvenirs—have become central to Stonehenge's existence. Visitors include the massive free- and fringe-festivals and fairs held at the site over the last thirty years, which have generated enormous controversy and set the context for a national British debate about who controls and can use the area. Bender (1998) has observed that the demands of some to freely tramp about the site are pitted against the desires of others to fence off the place in preservation and safeguard Stonehenge as a constructive, informative, and educational monument. However, it should also be noted that the history of tourism and fairs at the site goes much further back than recent visitor counts reflect. After all, the Royal Warrant of 1680 granted property owner Thomas Haywood the right to hold an annual fair at Stonehenge (Chippindale 1994).

Moreover, study of the past and preservation of artifacts have long been defined as recreational activities to be undertaken by curious visitors. Nowadays, there are numerous amateur archaeology clubs, popular archaeology books sell well, and scholars like Uzi Baram and Yorke Rowan (2004) note that tourism is a massive, global industry. But antiquarians and natural historians—the forerunners of today's professional historians, anthropologists, and archaeologists—were also men of leisure. They were men who had the ability to set time aside from economic burdens and social demands, to simply play among the past. Christopher Chippindale (1984) notes that early Stonehenge researchers and preservationists were individuals such as eighteenth-century-physician William Stuckeley. Stuckeley served as the first secretary of the Society of Antiquaries in London and found time apart from his medical practice each summer to survey and measure the site. His participation is part of a grand tradition. Archaeologists of all stripes have had an extensive history of working with amateurs and today most consider volunteer and amateur participation integral to the preservation of archaeological resources (Sabloff 1998).

However, the henge is but one part of Stonehenge II. The two moai are connected to yet another recreational tradition—that of tiki culture. When Alfred Shepperd erected Easter Island heads at the site, he was directly linking it to an American concept of leisure. Tikis are, in the narrow sense, the anthropomorphic images from Oceania—such as the massive heads of Easter Island. However, Douglas Nason (2001) explains that tiki has broadened out and now serves as a confluence of Oceanic culture, artifacts from the Pacific region, and a particularly American sense of kitsch. Tikis are now identified as symbols of recreation.

Tiki-as-recreation began in the 1930s with restaurants like Don the Beachcomber's in Hollywood, California, continued through the1940s with American soldiers returning from the South Pacific and the popularity of James Michener's writing, and blossomed mid-twentieth century with archaeologist Thor Heyerdahl's rafting across

Figure 6.6 Tiki Resurgance and Global Reach

The heyday of tiki-as-recreation culture unfolded mid-twentieth century. But a 1990s resurgence in tiki continues into the new millennium. Tiki's role and reach are reflected in these artifacts: a drink coaster from Trader Vic's tiki-themed restaurant (collected at the Chicago location in November 2003) and an advertisement for Burt's Tiki Lounge in Albuquerque, New Mexico, from the weekly newspaper The Alibi (January 12–18, 2006, p. 38).

the Pacific, a proliferation of Polynesian-themed dinner clubs, and jet travel to the new state of Hawaii (Kirsten 2000). Douglas Nason (2001) explains that Leroy Schmaltz and Bob Van Oosting became key figures in the promotion of a tiki lifestyle when they formed the Oceanic Arts design house in Whittier, California, in 1956. The firm designed and built numerous tiki-themed locales—such as Disneyland's Enchanted Tiki Room—based on carvings from across the Pacific. Schmaltz and Van Oosting set the standard for tiki culture. By 1968, the reach of Oceanic Arts and tiki-as-recreation had extended so far that Schmaltz and Van Oosting actually imported tiki sculptures *to* Papeetee, Tahiti for a tourist hotel (Anonymous 1968:3).

Pacific cultural artifacts had become entwined with an American proclivity for eating, drinking, and a vacation from social responsibilities. Tiki meant recreation. Sven Kirsten (2000:39–40) notes that, by the 1960s, tiki culture defined a recreational lifestyle for a generation of Americans in which:

> Polynesian parties provided the outlet that allowed the man in the grey flannel suit to regress to a rule-free primitive naivety: Donning colorful aloha shirts (which did not have to be tucked in!), getting intoxicated by sweet exotic concoctions with names that resembled a lilting infant idiom (Lapu Lapu, Mauna Loa Puki), eating luau pig with bare hands, and engaging in hula and limbo contests provided the opportunity to cut loose and have fun in an otherwise conservative society.

No tiki room was complete without an anthropomorphic carving, and cocktails with names like the "Headhunter" were best served in glasses shaped like the Rapa Nui moai (Kirsten 2000).

The abundance of dinner clubs and luaus is looked back on by many today as a historical moment, and the number and extravagance of Polynesian-themed establishments have waned since a late-1960s peak (Kirsten 2000). Yet, tiki culture and its concordant images remain vibrant symbols of American leisure. In the 1990s, a new school of tiki developed alongside the generational resurgence in lounge culture. People rediscovered Oceanic arts. The artist Shag painted his popular *"Night of the Tiki"* series, and tiki bars once again started catering to a new generation of U.S. pleasure seekers (Nason 2001). Tiki continues to be firmly equated with recreation and playful abandon in the American, if not global, psyche (figure 6.6).

Alfred Shepperd aligned his construction with these Stonehenge and tiki strands of recreation and leisure. He had visited the originals in the leisure of his own retirement and experienced their attraction first hand. Shepperd knew that he was dealing with traditions well suited to catch the positive attention that he sought from passing motorists. He built Stonehenge II on a solid foundation of recreation.

Experience instead of Education

Although Shepperd engaged with lasting traditions of leisure, he didn't make exact copies of those megalithic sites he knew of and had visited. He wasn't trying to replicate the originals so much as replicate their powerful presence. Visual or physical experience is primary over educational or intellectual understanding at Stonehenge II. This separates it from other replicas and officially sanctioned archaeological and historic sites. Most heavily visited sites present a story alongside the artifacts. The stewards of the original Stonehenge in England try to offer an explanatory experience—the focus of much current controversy surrounding the site—based on a context constructed from guide books, dioramas, instructional signs, and a visitor center (Bender 1998). Even other out-of-place archaeological replicas across the western United States, such as the fake Anasazi ruins at Manitou Springs, Colorado (discussed in Chapter Three) leverage explanatory authority and specifically attempt to educate the visitor. But Stonehenge II offers little pretense of education about either itself or the stone originals back in England and Easter Island. No context has been developed around this site. The sign introducing the site explains less than the mystery it adds (see figure 6.5). There is no archaeological or ethnographic explanation linking the site to the either prehistoric British or Pacific cultures, nor even an attempt to present an entirely accurate model. The family-run website, which does explain some of how Stonehenge II was built, is not accessible or even advertised on location. Stonehenge II simply lacks the basic corollary information that is easily accessible to visitors of most popular archaeological sites.

Playing with the Past

The appeal of Alfred Shepperd's creation rests on more than just symbols of recreation. The lack of explanatory context indicates that something else is going on here. It is evident that Stonehenge II is arranged for physically visiting and viewing first-hand. It is evident that the site is particularly attractive in and of itself. Thus, the site is best understood for its personal-level discursive and expressive qualities. Shepperd and Hill were savvy builders who recognized the power of western landscapes. They were skilled at manipulating various materials and saw obvious potential in the use of archaeological icons. Shepperd meticulously mowed and added to his original stone to make passersby take notice. He clearly conceived of the power in the incongruity of object and place. He fostered an unmitigated participatory experience. It is clear that visitors to the site, through their actions, understand this. Local newspaperman Jeff Davis, writing on the Shepperd family website (2001:no page number), explains: "You can play among the standing stones. Hide-and-seek is the most common game of choice, but tag and other children's pastimes are possible. Most important of all, use your imagination. Transport yourself to a distant land, a distant time."

Visitors are directed to play instead of participating in a structured and explicitly educational experience. However, this does not mean that play among the megaliths lacks formative power. Anthropologist Don Handelman (1974:67) defines play as, "as a general rubric of 'unserious' behavior which subsumes what are termed jokes, joking activity, horseplay, pranks and games." Handelman (1974:67) notes that, "play is by definition 'unserious' activity, and therefore its communicative content does not have to be reacted to seriously at the time of its transmission." However, he goes on to explain that—even in situations lacking seriousness—important messages about how the world works and how people should approach it are still transferred and received in the process of play. Things need not be only stuffy and self-serious to have importance.

Historian Philip Deloria (1998) has shown how significant the act of play with primitives and others has been in shaping American consciousness. Deloria's (1998:184) review of two centuries of Americans—both adults and children—playing with the primitive and exotic nature of Native Americans shows that, "play was powerful, for it not only made meanings, it made them *real* . . . identity was not so much imagined as it was performed, materialized through one's body." Likewise, play among the stones of Stonehenge II stimulates the senses. It puts the body in motion and in perspective.

Phenomenology and the Presence of the Past

Stonehenge II encourages play. The site engages the entire body, offers the opportunity for a bodily comparison of scale, and bridges the divide between object and individual. Archaeologists are experienced with the ways in which artifacts on a landscape can affect people. We study this process from the perspective of phenomenology. Phenomenology, according to archaeologist Christopher Tilley (2004:1), "involves the attempt to describe the objects of consciousness in the manner in which they are presented to the consciousness. It attempts to reveal the world as it is experienced directly by a subject as opposed to how we might theoretically assume it to be."

Philosopher Maurice Merleau-Ponty (1962) grounds phenomenology in the human body. The body is seen as a physical thing that operates within a wider world and is a condition of how we experience that wider world. According to phenomenology, people are not able to take an outside or objective perspective of the world (Tilley 2004). We are not disembodied minds somehow separate from, or outside of, our corporeal being. This means that the body and its senses are the basis for our experiences. Our bodies are the scales we use for understanding the world which people inhabit. So, when people encounter an object, our knowledge of that thing is grounded in the relationship between it and our bodies. Thus, artifacts have an influence on us because of how they relate to us. The idea that artifacts have influence may appear similar to archaeologist David Hurst Thomas's (2002:132) concept of "unembellished anthropological things"—those human-made artifacts that seem so clear as to present their own reality (discussed in Chapter 3).

But a phenomenological perspective is more refined and centers the influence on a relationship, not a thing itself. It shows that we have specific relationships with artifacts because our bodies are the points of engagement with them, not because artifacts somehow speak for themselves. A phenomenological perspective is especially useful to archaeologists because, as Tilley (2004) explains, specific artifacts and particular places clearly have the same abilities to affect us today as they had on people in the past.

Big and Solid Things on a Landscape

A phenomenological perspective highlights certain sets of interactions between people's bodies and megaliths. In fact, Tilley wrote *The Materiality of Stone* (2004) from a phenomenological viewpoint, specifically about the ways that people engage with megaliths. He examined the material nature of different megaliths and compiled ways in which people interact with them. For instance, a menhir's lack of smell (unlike organic wood structures) or a stone's silence (solid forms lack echo or resonance when struck) was seen to have significance in relation to qualities of timelessness. Further, when Tilley looked at megaliths from different angles, he noted that some have shapes that seem firmly rooted into the soil, whereas others (primarily those with convex or concave curves) appear to possess kinetic potential. They give the impression that they are growing or moving out of the ground around them, instead of appearing static. Of course, one of the most obvious uses of the body is as a scale of artifact size. Tilley (2004:6) explains that, "natural and cultural things of significant height (mountains, cliffs, waterfalls, church spires, buildings, stones, ceramic vessels, monuments) most usually impress and we find them awe inspiring as they relate to the physicality of our bodies." Folklorist Susan Stewart (1993) says that gigantic objects miniaturize us and make people feel toy-like when we use our bodies as scales. Towering megaliths stir up strong emotions.

However, individual artifacts are not alone in provoking strong feelings. Stewart (1993) also explains that gigantic things thrust the body into an exterior place because we fall under a giant's shadow. We are limited to experiencing only small pieces of large objects at any one moment, and we know them as a whole only when we move around to gain other perspectives. Entire landscapes are thus open for us to engage with. Of course, landscapes also offer the opportunity to interact with more than just one object. We may run across multiple objects in our movements and have particular experiences based on their arrangements and alignments. Tilley (2004) notes that landscapes are not something we simply look at or think about, but things which we live though and define ourselves upon. For him, landscapes are potent mediums for socialization and knowledge. The ways in which we are able to move our bodies through a landscape—and what we engage there—has profound effects on us.

Figure 6.7 At Play among the Fake Stones
Visitors are encouraged to play among, on top of, and next to the megaliths at Stonehenge II. Here, play is an experience that engages the entire body and all the senses.

Stonehenge II, Phenomenology, and Play

Descriptions of phenomenology and the idea of a body engaging an entire landscape may seem particularly self-serious and abstract subjects. However, the hands-on act of engagement doesn't necessarily weigh people down. We shouldn't forget that Stonehenge II is so unabashedly out of place that visitors intuitively *play* among the stones.

That which draws the passing motorists also holds their interest once they stop. Visitors run between the megaliths and play with their shadows (figure 6.7). They compare their own bodies to the outrageous size and form of the moai—the results of which are laughable (figure 6.8). Visitors can feel the texture, mass, and shape of the megaliths when they lay themselves across what so clearly seems to be an altar stone—perhaps even a sacrificial one (figure 6.3)! The whorls and ridges sculpted into the trilithons feel rough to the touch. But when visitors step back from—better yet—actually lie down under the arches they get another perspective. The indented surface of the megaliths now form patterns like those found in the game of looking for animal and anthropomorphic shapes in the clouds. The megaliths tower over people in the same ways that Tilley (2004) recorded at European sites. But, of course, in south Texas the stones ring hollow when hands knock on them, and visitors can't help but enjoy the incongruity of it all. And, indeed, this is an entire, multi-faceted landscape with ample opportunities for engagement. Running or causally strolling the flat lawn back and forth between the heads and the henges is a fantastical game of travel—from the British Isles to the South Pacific—without ever having left Texas.

Strange Things Are Interesting

Christopher Tilley (2004) explains that knowledge of an object's history plays an important role in the ways in which physical things affect people. A phenomenological perspective is one in which the mind isn't disembodied, but this doesn't mean that knowledge has no role. For instance, knowing the origin of the stones used in megaliths, "was a 'hidden' dimension to their meaning and potency" (Tilley 2004:36). Knowing that a stone might have been collected from a great distance or from a particular prominence is meaningful to both prehistoric and present peoples. Similarly, there is also power in not knowing.

Figure 6.8 The Scale of the Body

The massive scale and sheer presence of the heads at Stonehenge II (approximately 3.5 m in height) is conceived of in bodily terms. These tiki tower over visitors, but their exaggerated features produce genuinely humorous comparisons as well. Jeff Fox (quoted in Nason 2001:24–25) explains that:

> The tiki's ability to transform itself into so many different forms while still holding onto a tiny part of its original meaning has allowed it to transcend many cultures and much time. A wooden tiki carved in the traditional Oceanic style and a pop culture regurgitation of a tiki are very different, obviously. But the recurring idea behind both kinds of tikis is that they are representations of man. This speaks to our innate fascination with cultures different from our own.

155

Stonehenge II is attractive, in part, because it allows for mystery and speculation. Visitors are affected by the fact that they aren't privy to knowledge. Not knowing allows play to include speculation and stories of what-if and how-so. Of course, there are also the visitors—a majority of visitors—who at least recognize that south Texas prehistory was never host to megalithic heads and henges like those found at Stonehenge II. Incongruity is, for them, a particular and meaningful kind of historical knowledge as well. Experiencing incongruity is part of the site's essential joke. Incongruity helps make Stonehenge II such an attractive place in which to play.

Authenticity and Experience

The phenomenological approach to artifacts and landscapes places value on experiencing authentic objects in their native environments. Both Christopher Tilley (2004) and Susan Stewart (1993) stress the importance of first-hand, in-context experiences. They emphasize that the body engages representations of things differently from how it interacts with actual objects. This is especially true of pictures, narrative descriptions, or souvenirs. These things may evoke memories of your experiences, but you aren't exactly reliving them. The idea that people today can have experiences similar to people in the past—for instance, that a megalith dwarfed them and continues to dwarf us—is predicated on shared context (Tilley 2004). Tilley and Stewart both view pictures, narrative descriptions, and souvenirs as inauthentic, out of context replicas of authentic things. But, Stonehenge II isn't just a replica and just because it isn't in England or Easter Island doesn't mean it's out of context. We can still use phenomenological approaches to understand what's going on here.

Perhaps counter-intuitively, Stonehenge II is a fake that provides real experiences. It exists in its own right, according to the peculiarities of its place. Stonehenge II is neither merely a representation of megalithic originals nor a physical souvenir brought back from travels to megalithic sites. Alfred Shepperd had traveled, but he didn't just bring those sites back. He reshaped ideas about them according to his home and life in Texas. He built his own site based on the happenstance of the limestone slab that his neighbor had given him as a gift. Certainly, Shepperd incorporated the experiences of his own trips into his construction. But he also dealt with the layout of his property in relation to the adjacent highway and the specific ways in which he might catch the attention of passing motorists. He had to consider how large to make the megaliths. He had to find the links between the moai's top knots and the cowboy's ten-gallon hat. He had to decide how the heads and henges could be aligned on his own lawn. Of course, Alfred Shepperd wasn't the first individual to erect a megalith. He clearly took knowledge from other megalithic sites. But, then again, the numerous people who contributed to Stonehenge in England or erected the moai on Easter Island weren't the first either.

Stonehenge II is inauthentic archaeology. It contains no authentic prehistoric artifacts. It isn't even an especially accurate re-creation of megalithic sites or archaeological landscapes. But a phenomenological perspective shows that the site's visitors do have meaningful experiences. Stonehenge II was built on two solid foundations: the traditions of recreation and leisure that people associate with megaliths and the materiality of a large, imposing, and incongruous place. The site is part of grand recreational tradition and offers visitors a place to play. Simply being at Stonehenge II is an unmitigated and interesting experience that engages the entire body. Playing at Stonehenge II is fun, and sometimes archaeology is too much fun to worry about.

References and Further Reading

Anonymous
1968   "Made in Whittier" Tikis Will Greet Tourists in Tahiti. *The Daily News* (Whittier, California) August 30:3.

Baram, U. and Y. Rowan
2004   Archaeology after Nationalism: Globalization and the Consumption of the Past. In *Marketing Heritage: Archaeology and the Consumption of the Past*. Y. Rowan and U. Baram, editors. AltaMira, Walnut Creek, California.

Bender, B.
1998   *Stonehenge: Making Space*. Berg, Oxford, England.

Carlson, P.
2006   Jurassic Lark: What Do Dinosaurs and the Civil War Have in Common? Mark Cline's Art. *The Washington Post* April 24:C01.

Chippindale, C.
1987   *Stonehenge Observed: Images from 1350 to 1987*. City Art Gallery, Southhampton, England.
1994   *Stonehenge Complete*. Thames and Hudson, London.

Cope, J.
1992   *Jehovahkill*. Polygram Records, New York.

Daniels, G.
1959   Some Megalithic Follies. *Antiquity* 33(132):282–284.

Deloria, P.J.
1998   *Playing Indian*. Yale University Press, New Haven, Connecticut.

Handelman, D.
1974   A Note on Play. *American Anthropologist* 76(1):66–68.

Kirsten, S.A.
2000   *The Book of Tiki: The Cult of Polynesian Pop in Fifties America*. Taschen America LLC., New York.

McLeod, G.A.
1995   *Day Trips, Vol. 1: Texas Tours, Maps & Photos*. Austin Chronicle Corporation, Austin, Texas.

Merleau-Ponty, M.
1962   *The Phenomenology of Perception*. Routledge, London.

Michell, J.
1982   *Megalithomania: Artists, Antiquarians and Archaeologists at the Old Stone Monuments*. Cornell University Press, Ithaca, New York.

Nason, D.A.
2001   *Night of the Tiki: The Art of Shag, Schmaltz and Selected Primitive Oceanic Carvings*. Last Gasp, San Francisco.

Rahtz, P. and I. Burrows
1992   Archaeology Is Too Important a Subject Not to Be Joked About. *Archaeological Review from Cambridge* 11(2):373–387.

Sabloff, J.A.
1998   Distinguished Lecture in Archeology: Communication and the Future of American Archaeology. *American Anthropologist* 100(4):869–875.

Shepperd, A.L.
2001   *Stonehenge II*. http://www.alfredshepperd.com/stonehenge/untitled.html.

Stewart, S.
1993   *On Longing: Narratives of the Miniature, the Gigantic, the Souvenir, the Collection*. Duke University Press, Durham, North Carolina.

Thomas, D.H.
2002   Roadside Ruins: Does America Still Need Archaeology Museums? In *Public Benefits of Archaeology*, B. Little, editor. University Press of Florida, Gainesville.

Tilley, C.
2004   *The Materiality of Stone: Explorations in Landscape Phenomenology*. Berg, Oxford, the United Kingdom.

Critical Questions and Exercises

1. Humor, joking, and games are all attractive forces. In fact, archaeologists Philip Rahtz and Ian Burrows (1992:373) have declared that "archaeology is too important a subject not to be joked about." Have you ever seen archaeology presented in especially fun or playful ways? Or have you been subjected to only stern and severe presentations of the past? Consider the books (including textbooks) you've read, the movies and television you've watched, and the signs and displays that you might have seen at museums and archaeology sites. Even examine the personalities of any archaeologists you've actually met. For instance, do you find evidence of artist Mark Dion's statement, back in Chapter 5 of this book, that many European archaeologists know that it's hard for them to access and use humor, irony, or parody in their professional work? Does professional archaeology appear to offer opportunities for unabashed play like the nonprofessional archaeology of Stonehenge II? What might your own observations indicate about how professional archaeology operates?

2. Examine how you've used your own body to experience the materiality of the past. Have you been to a place like Stonehenge II or original megalithic sites like those in England and Easter Island? Have you had the opportunity—at an archaeology site, while visiting a museum, or simply traveling through the world around you—to experience physical artifacts in their original contexts? List the ways in which you interact with physical objects. Then, contrast your experiences to what you've read about the people who use their whole bodies to play at Stonehenge II.

INDEX

ABOUT THE AUTHOR

Troy Lovata graduated cum laude with a bachelor's of arts degree in anthropology from Colorado State University. He holds master's and doctorate degrees in anthropology, with a focus on the visual presentation of archaeology, from The University of Texas. Lovata is an assistant professor in the University Honors Program at the University of New Mexico. He previously served as a senior lecturer in the Technology, Literacy and Culture Program at The University of Texas. He also serves, by appointment of the mayor, on the Arts Board of Albuquerque, New Mexico.